**New Directions for Student Services**

Elizabeth J. Whitt
EDITOR-IN-CHIEF

John H. Schuh
ASSOCIATE EDITOR

# Angst and Hope: Current Issues in Student Affairs Leadership

Elizabeth J. Whitt
Larry D. Roper
Kent T. Porterfield
Jill E. Carnaghi
EDITORS

Number 153 • Spring 2016
Jossey-Bass
San Francisco

ANGST AND HOPE: CURRENT ISSUES IN STUDENT AFFAIRS LEADERSHIP
Elizabeth J. Whitt, Larry D. Roper, Kent T. Porterfield, Jill E. Carnaghi (eds.)
New Directions for Student Services, no. 153

Elizabeth J. Whitt, Editor-in-Chief
John H. Schuh, Associate Editor

Copyright © 2016 Wiley Periodicals, Inc., A Wiley Company. All rights reserved. No part of this publication may be reproduced in any form or by any means, except as permitted under section 107 or 108 of the 1976 United States Copyright Act, without either the prior written permission of the publisher or authorization through the Copyright Clearance Center, 222 Rosewood Drive, Danvers, MA 01923; (978) 750-8400; fax (978) 646-8600. The copyright notice appearing at the bottom of the first page of an article in this journal indicates the copyright holder's consent that copies may be made for personal or internal use, or for personal or internal use of specific clients, on the condition that the copier pay for copying beyond that permitted by law. This consent does not extend to other kinds of copying, such as copying for general distribution, for advertising or promotional purposes, for creating collective works, or for resale. Such permission requests and other permission inquiries should be addressed to the Permissions Department, c/o John Wiley & Sons, Inc., 111 River St., Hoboken, NJ 07030; (201) 748-8789, fax (201) 748-6326, www.wiley.com/go/permissions.

NEW DIRECTIONS FOR STUDENT SERVICES (ISSN 0164-7970, e-ISSN 1536-0695) is part of The Jossey-Bass Higher and Adult Education Series and is published quarterly by Wiley Subscription Services, Inc., A Wiley Company, at Jossey-Bass, One Montgomery Street, Suite 1200, San Francisco, CA 94104-4594. POSTMASTER: Send address changes to New Directions for Student Services, Jossey-Bass, One Montgomery Street, Suite 1200, San Francisco, CA 94104-4594.

*New Directions for Student Services* is indexed in CIJE: Current Index to Journals in Education (ERIC), Contents Pages in Education (T&F), Current Abstracts (EBSCO), Education Index /Abstracts (H.W. Wilson), Educational Research Abstracts Online (T&F), ERIC Database (Education Resources Information Center), and Higher Education Abstracts (Claremont Graduate University).

Microfilm copies of issues and articles are available in 16 mm and 35 mm, as well as microfiche in 105 mm, through University Microfilms Inc., 300 North Zeeb Road, Ann Arbor, Michigan 48106-1346.

SUBSCRIPTIONS cost $89 for individuals in the U.S., Canada, and Mexico, and $113 in the rest of the world for print only; $89 in all regions for electronic only; and $98 in the U.S., Canada, and Mexico for combined print and electronic; and $122 for combined print and electronic in the rest of the world. Institutional print only subscriptions are $335 in the U.S., $375 in Canada and Mexico, and $409 in the rest of the world; electronic only subscriptions are $335 in all regions; and combined print and electronic subscriptions are $402 in the U.S., $442 in Canada and Mexico, and $476 in the rest of the world.

EDITORIAL CORRESPONDENCE should be sent to the Editor-in-Chief, Elizabeth J. Whitt, University of California Merced, 5200 North Lake Rd. Merced, CA 95343.

Cover design: Wiley
Cover Images: © Lava 4 images | Shutterstock

www.josseybass.com

# Contents

Editors' Notes 5
*Elizabeth J. Whitt, Larry D. Roper, Kent T. Porterfield, Jill E. Carnaghi*

1. Past, Present, and Future: Contexts for Current Challenges and Opportunities for Student Affairs Leadership 9
*Kent T. Porterfield, Elizabeth J. Whitt*
Contexts for identifying and understanding current opportunities and challenges for student affairs leaders are described and a framework for the rest of the sourcebook is offered.

2. What Troubles You? What Keeps You up at Night? 19
*Larry D. Roper, Elizabeth J. Whitt*
Responses of student affairs leaders to questions about the challenges and obstacles they face in their work are examined and discussed.

3. What Excites You? What Keeps You Going? 39
*Elizabeth J. Whitt, Jill E. Carnaghi*
Responses of student affairs leaders to questions about the opportunities and joy they find in their work are examined and discussed.

4. Embracing Core Values: Finding Joy in the Challenges of our Work 55
*Larry D. Roper, Kent T. Porterfield, Elizabeth J. Whitt, Jill E. Carnaghi*
This chapter describes and discusses implications of the experiences of student affairs leaders—the challenges and the opportunities, the obstacles and the joy—for understanding and facilitating student affairs leadership.

Index 69

Appendices 73

# Editors' Notes

The idea for this sourcebook came from our individual and collective experiences in student affairs and our collective interest in looking back and looking ahead at the nature of student affairs work. Our professional careers in higher education and student affairs span most of the past five decades, so there is considerable looking back we could do! In addition, all of us have experience as senior student affairs administrators, three of us at both private and public institutions, one of us at a private college; all of us have held leadership roles in student affairs professional associations, including examinations of future trends and challenges for student affairs; all of us have taught courses in student affairs preparation programs and two of us are full professors in academic departments at research universities. And all of us still are actively engaged in the scholarship and practice of student affairs and undergraduate education.

Once we had committed to prepare a *New Directions for Student Services* sourcebook about current trends, opportunities, and challenges for senior student affairs leaders, we identified a number of approaches to that topic, many of which are reflected in the final product. What issues must be addressed? Should we look at student affairs organizations? Student affairs leadership? Trends in external demands that influence student affairs officers? Trends internal to colleges and universities? And how does the past affect the present? There were many directions we could go and issues we could tackle; the choices seemed almost limitless. But we also wanted whatever we produced to be useful (or, at least, interesting) to student affairs leaders.

As we considered options for the focus of the sourcebook, it occurred to us that we ought to start with the people who are on the ground, the people who are facing those opportunities and challenges every day: senior student affairs professionals. But what did we need to know, and from whom?

## What Do (Some) Student Affairs Leaders Think?

We decided that if we were going to start with the leaders, we ought to do so in a way that let them speak for themselves and not to our preconceptions. But how might we do that in a way that did not create unreasonable demands on their time? Finally, we hit on the idea of contacting them by e-mail and asking two brief open-ended questions: (a) "What troubles you? What keeps you up at night" and (b) "What excites you? What keeps you going?" We did not know what responses those questions would elicit, but we hoped they would be provocative for the people we contacted.

For specific information about our study process, including participant selection and characteristics and data collection and analysis, please see

Appendix A. What follows here is a very brief summary, for the purposes of providing context for the rest of this sourcebook.

We contacted 70 senior student affairs officers in September 2015. The sample was neither random nor representative; instead, we sought a mix of professional experiences, institutional type, geographic distribution in the United States.

We received responses to our questions from 53 of the 70 people we contacted, a 75% response rate, which surprised and pleased us. The 53 (identified in Appendix B) provided the breadth of experience we had hoped for, though, unfortunately, about half of the nonrespondents were senior leaders at private colleges and universities.

The leaders' responses filled about 40 single-spaced pages, almost two-thirds of which—we were interested to note—focused on what troubled them (Note: You can find the verbatim responses, with identifying information removed, in Appendix C and Appendix D). Their answers were expected and unexpected, and, as we had hoped, both interesting and provocative.

We analyzed the data within and across the broad questions, a process that yielded the themes that follow. Although the themes are listed as though they are discrete, we recognize they are not. Instead, they are interrelated, shaping one another in complicated ways that might differ by campus. So, for example, access to success is likely to be inextricably linked to campus climates for diversity and inclusion, as well as students' health and well-being.

## Themes: What Troubles You? What Keeps You up at Night?

1. Affordability and access (including affordability of higher education to students and families; access to success, not just admission; access to high-quality and high-impact learning experiences; gaps in achievement and attainment).
2. Student health and well-being (including mental health challenges and services, campus and student safety, campus resources to support student health and wellness).
3. Diversity and inclusion (including cultures and climates for diversity and inclusion; inclusive communities; concerns and demands regarding civility, free speech, and discourse of differences; student activism regarding inclusion; multiple and intersecting identities).
4. Regulations and compliance (including discourse about the value of higher education; external mandates, regulations, and political agendas; perceived conflicts between regulations and compliance and learning and education).
5. Technology and media (including influences on campuses of 24-hr news cycle and social media; climates of crisis, urgency, and instant gratification)

6. Student affairs (including roles, perceptions of competence, preparation and experiences, effectiveness of student affairs leadership, models of organization and practice, use of evidence and data to inform decisions).

Most of the responses to "What troubles you?" were framed by concerns about resources; that is, these issues were troubling, in part, because of limited and declining financial and human resources. Therefore, instead of treating resources as a separate theme, we have discussed it in the text of the sourcebook as a critical context for what troubles the respondents.

## Themes: What Excites You? What Keeps You Going?

1. Students (including students as the center of the work, facilitating student learning and success, spending time with students, learning from students).
2. Making a difference (including the transformative powers of education, creating and sustaining inclusive communities, promoting social justice and equity, uses of digital technologies and social media).
3. Collaboration and community (including partnerships on and off campus, extending campus borders, teamwork, professional and civic engagement).
4. Leading and facilitating change (including institutional change and effectiveness, creating transformative organizations, engaging with the academic mission to create seamless learning environments, contributions of student affairs to institutional effectiveness, leading change).
5. Learning, data, and scholarship (including being a learner; outcomes assessment and program evaluation; using data, theories, and scholarship for decision making; staying current).
6. "I love my job": Ultimately, it's all about all the work (including joy, hope, core values and principles, the whole of "what keeps me going").

## Overview of the Sourcebook

The six themes about "What troubles you?" are described and discussed in Chapter 2 and the six themes about "What keeps you going?" are discussed in Chapter 3. Chapter 1 provides a general context for considering current challenges and opportunities for student affairs leaders, including a brief look backward at what has, and has not, changed. In Chapter 4, we address the similarities and differences in the data across the themes and questions and offer some propositions regarding the implications of what we learned from the respondents for current and future student affairs leadership.

We close these notes with a message of deep gratitude for the generosity of our respondents in taking time to share their experiences with us. We hope this sourcebook conveys those experiences in ways the student affairs leaders recognize.

> Elizabeth J. Whitt
> Larry D. Roper
> Kent T. Porterfield
> Jill E. Carnaghi
> Editors

ELIZABETH J. WHITT *is vice provost and dean for undergraduate education and professor in sociology at University of California, Merced.*

LARRY D. ROPER *is professor in the school of language, culture and society at Oregon State University and coordinator, College Student Services Administration and Social Justice Minor.*

KENT T. PORTERFIELD *is vice president for student development at Saint Louis University.*

JILL E. CARNAGHI *is assistant vice president for student development at Saint Louis University.*

**1**

*Contexts for identifying and understanding current opportunities and challenges for student affairs leaders are described and a framework for the rest of the sourcebook is offered.*

# Past, Present, and Future: Contexts for Current Challenges and Opportunities for Student Affairs Leadership

*Kent T. Porterfield, Elizabeth J. Whitt*

> "We have never faced as many difficult challenges [in higher education] as we do today."
>
> "So in a word, Yes. Higher education is most assuredly in crisis."

It might (or might not) be surprising to know those statements are not part of a single assertion and were, in fact, written two decades apart. The first statement was by Robert Atwell at the time of his retirement from the American Council on Education in 1994. As he reflected on his 40-year career in American higher education, Atwell asserted that, in all that time, "we have never faced as many difficult challenges as we do today" (Atwell, 1994, p. 125). Among the difficult challenges he and others described in the 1990s were unprecedented diversity of students seeking higher education; rapid advances in, and expansion of, electronic technologies; waning public confidence in higher education, accompanied by increasing calls for accountability for institutional effectiveness and student learning outcomes; and shrinking financial resources, especially from public sources, accompanied by increases in tuition and reductions in federal support for student financial aid (American College Personnel Association [ACPA], 1994; ACPA and National Association of Student Personnel Administrators [NASPA], 1997; Andreas & Schuh, 1999). In their discussion of these and other challenges facing higher education in general and student affairs in particular, Rosalind Andreas and John Schuh said—with, perhaps, some understatement—"Few would characterize the 1990s as a 'Golden Age' for postsecondary education" in the United States (Andreas & Schuh, 1999, p. 1). A long list of reports calling for reforms in higher education, especially with regard to undergraduate student learning and success, supported that assertion (see American Association for Higher Education [AAHE], ACPA, & NASPA, 1998; ACPA, 1994; ACPA & NASPA, 1997; Boyer Commission on Educating Undergraduates in the Research University, 1998; Johnson & Cheatham, 1999; National Association of State Universities and Land-Grant Colleges [NASULGC], 1997, 1999, 2000).

The second statement was written by Goldie Blumenstyk, senior writer at *The Chronicle of Higher Education*, in 2015. She posed the question, "Is higher education in America in crisis?," then surveyed the current landscape to reach her answer: "So in a word, Yes. Higher education is most assuredly in crisis" (Blumenstyk, 2015, p. 1). Elements of that landscape of crisis included the following:

> Over the past thirty years, the price of college has gone up ... Student debt is at an all-time high ... Doubts about the value of college are on the rise. State support for the public sector ... has yet to (and may never) return to the generous levels of the early 2000s ... Collectively, colleges reflect—some say even amplify—the racial and income inequities of the nation's neighborhoods ... And a restless reform movement, inspired by the promise of new technology and backed by powerful political and financial might is growing more insistent that the enterprise spend less, show better results, and become more open to new kinds of educational providers. (Blumenstyk, 2015, p. 1)

It seems safe to conclude, then, that the middle of the second decade of the twenty-first century also is not a "golden age" for American higher education. As in the 1990s, contemporary calls for reform, including reform of undergraduate education, are plentiful and persistent (see American Association of Community Colleges, American Association of State Colleges and Universities [ASCU], & Association of Public and Land-Grant Universities [APLU], 2015; Arum & Roksa, 2011; Byrne, 2006; Carey, 2015; Craig, 2015; Keeling & Hersh, 2011; Lumina Foundation for Education, 2009; National Association of Student Personnel Administrators [NASPA] & ACPA, 2004; Shirky, 2014; Task Force on the Future of Student Affairs [Task Force], 2010; U.S. Department of Education, 2006; White House, 2013). In fact, we might wonder when that golden age was, as evidence of similar critiques and similar challenges can be found in higher education and student affairs literature well before the 1990s (see American Council on Education [ACE], 1937, 1949; ACPA, 1975; Appleton, Briggs, & Rhatigan, 1978; Brown, 1972; Kuh, Whitt, & Shedd, 1987; Lloyd-Jones, 1954; Mueller, 1961; Study Group on the Conditions of Excellence in American Higher Education, 1984).

That is a topic to which we return later in this chapter, the purpose of which is to describe and discuss the context for current student affairs leaders and their roles. As we stated in the Editors' Notes, this *New Directions for Student Services* sourcebook focuses on contemporary challenges and opportunities for student affairs leadership. The specific challenges and opportunities we examine were provided by a group of student affairs leaders (note: for simplicity, we refer to them hereafter as "the student affairs leaders" or "our respondents") in Fall 2015 (see the Appendices for information about those leaders and the data they provided). To consider the meaning and implications of those individuals' reflections and experiences for student affairs leadership at this point in time, we assume the context of those experiences—the current state of American higher education—is relevant. We also decided, however, to focus on the "student affairs" portion of the leaders' experiences, a decision that led us to take a brief look at historical and current trends in student affairs work.

We begin this chapter with additional information about the current state of American higher education. We then shift our perspective to student affairs work and examine its development by looking at some key documents in the history of student affairs. We conclude with a brief look at two perspectives on how the student affairs profession and student affairs leaders could respond to current trends.

## Current Context

As we noted above, critiques of American higher education from inside and outside the academy have sounded a consistent drumbeat of urgent needs for reform of current practices and structures for more than three decades. The content of the drumbeat has been just as consistent: increasing costs and declining funding, inadequate responses to shifting student and national demographics, new competitive economic demands, complex technological advancements, globalization, and increasing public skepticism that colleges and universities provide a quality return on investment.

There are certainly contemporary critics of higher education who raise the same concerns. For example, Clay Shirky (2014), consultant and educator on internet technologies, claims that colleges and universities are perfectly situated for a time that no longer exists: a time of rapid growth, elasticity in the price of tuition, homogenous student populations, and great institutional and system autonomy. He maintains that, as the economics of higher education changed, colleges and universities did not. Instead, we assumed an unlimited supply of students, continuing government funding levels for research, and a purely additive model of operating. As we grew beyond our resources, we made only the slightest of adjustments and spent decades trying to preserve and defend practices that have outlived the business model in which we continue to operate. In doing so, we have tested the patience of our public, as well as colleagues in the academy (Shirky, 2014). Our critics argue, and the facts are compelling, that colleges and universities in the Unites States are underserving the overwhelming number of citizens who need and desire postsecondary education, and we continue to place our bets on a system that works for fewer and fewer students. That is, the number of undergraduate students who attend college full time, live on campus, and require limited amounts of financial aid and academic support continues to dwindle.

At the same time, the importance of higher education has increased to the point that undergraduate education verges on a "requirement of a fully expressed citizenship" in contemporary society (Shapiro, 2005, p. 8). In a 2009 address to Congress, President Barack Obama asserted

> [Whatever] the training may be, every American will need to get more than a high school diploma ... That is why we will provide the support necessary for you to complete college and meet a new goal: by 2020, America will once again have the highest proportion of college graduates in the world. (Speech to the Joint Houses of Congress, February 24, 2009)

In 2013, President Obama announced "an ambitious new agenda" (White House Fact Sheet, August 22, 2013) to widen access to higher education by increasing affordability. This agenda was aimed at increasing institutional accountability for successful student outcomes by, among other things, establishing a ratings system that was intended to tie federal financial aid to institutional performance (e.g., graduation rates, community college transfer rates, earnings of graduates, student debt, and enrollment rates of low-income students) (Blumenstyk, 2015).

In 2015, the United States Department of Education claimed that college is no longer a luxury for the privileged, "but a necessity for individual economic opportunity and America's competitiveness in the global economy. At a time when jobs can go anywhere in the world, skills and education will determine success, for individuals and for nations" (retrieved from http://www.ed.gov/college). Nevertheless, the cost of attending college has been increasing at a significant rate for more than two decades. Consider that in 1993, the average debt per borrower in the nation's baccalaureate graduating class was below $10,000, whereas in 2015, the number is projected to be $35,000. In addition, in 1993 the percentage of students borrowing to pay for college was approximately 40%, in contrast to more than 70% in 2015. Simply put, more are borrowing and borrowing more (http://blogs.wsj.com/economics/2015/05/08/congratulations-class-of-2015-youre-the-most-indebted-ever-for-now/)

The characterizations of higher education in 2015 as "most assuredly in crisis" (Blumenstyk, 2015, p. 1), and, at the same time, "the greatest driver of social mobility in America" (U.S. Department of Education, 2015, retrieved from http://www.ed.gov/college) vividly illustrate the contemporary context of student affairs leaders. Potentially competing demands—providing high quality higher education that serves both individual and national needs to more and more diverse students; increasing financial, academic, and social support for those students; expanding institutional aspirations, goals, and responsibilities as resources shrink—create increasingly complex sets of challenges and opportunities for institutions and those who lead them. We come back to this complicated context at the end of this chapter and the end of this sourcebook, but, first we take a look at the development of the field of student affairs for additional understanding of student affairs leadership.

## "A Corrective Look Back"

We thank James Appleton, Channing Briggs, and James Rhatigan for a way to introduce our very brief examination of the development of student affairs work, particularly the values and principles of the field. Nearly 40 years ago, they offered a caveat to their colleagues:

> Few administrators see the relevance or importance of historical forces and issues to the present status of student affairs administration. This is a grievous miscalculation ... In our field, the present is a dominant preoccupation. The price of this preoccupation is the diminution not only of our predecessors but also of ourselves ... *We must understand that, in substantial ways, professional identity is rooted in the past.* (Appleton et al., 1978)

In 2009, ACPA and NASPA created a joint task force to look at current trends in higher education and develop recommendations for student affairs to respond to those trends. In doing so, the leading comprehensive student affairs associations followed a long tradition. At various critical points in the evolution of the student affairs field, groups of faculty members and administrators gathered to think carefully about the nature of student affairs work and its relevance to higher education and the institutions student affairs professionals served. Their work yielded reports and recommendations for moving forward.

For the purposes of this sourcebook, we feature (a) *Student Personnel Point of View* (ACE, 1937), (b) *Tomorrow's Higher Education (T.H.E.) Project* (ACPA, 1975; Brown, 1972), (c) *Student Learning Imperative* (ACPA, 1994), and (d) *Principles of Good Practice for Student Affairs* (ACPA & NASPA, 1997; Blimling, Whitt, and Associates, 1999). We could have selected other similar reports, but chose these for discussion here for two reasons. First, each was created at a time of thoroughgoing change in American higher education: (a) the period between the World Wars; (b) the period of rapid expansion and social and political foment at the end of the 1960s; and (c and d), the period of critical scrutiny of the effectiveness of higher education in general and undergraduate education in particular, as well as a crisis in public funding of higher education (Task Force, 2010). One could argue we are in such a period today. Second, as we sought to understand the challenges and opportunities facing current student affairs leaders, we were drawn to these documents' eloquent statements of the core values and principles of the student affairs field.

Looking across the four projects and the documents they produced, we saw consistent statements about what matters in student affairs work—about the principles that underlie and motivate that work. And we saw this consistency even though the *T.H.E Project* was "an attempt to reconceptualize college student affairs work ... a systematic change in the fundamental conceptions ... that will characterize our future professional practice" (ACPA, 1975, p. 333). Despite the 60 years spanned by these efforts and the differences in the circumstances of change that prompted them, the core values of student affairs work were described in much the same ways in each:

1. Student affairs work is about students, and their growth, learning, and development.
2. Student affairs professionals facilitate student learning and development by
   - grounding their work in the mission and goals of their institutions
   - building campus and community partnerships to create seamless learning and living environments
   - advocating for students and their needs
   - contributing to scholarship and research about students
   - creating and assessing learning outcomes to inform and improve practices, programs, and policies
   - promoting diversity, social justice, and inclusive communities through programs, practices, and policies
   - increasing access to higher education and success for all students.

As we discuss in more detail in Chapter 4, those core values provided a helpful framework for identifying the meaning and implications of the data our respondents provided.

**Back to the Present and the Future**

The final report of the ACPA-NASPA Task Force on the Future of Student Affairs, *Envisioning the Future of Student Affairs*, was released in February 2010. The Task Force called for rethinking student affairs work in light of major challenges confronting American higher education, including globalization, new demands for education, gaps in degree attainment and academic achievement, expanding technologies, and economic fluctuations. Rethinking student affairs, according to the Task Force, included the need to redefine roles and structures, focus on success for *all* students, build partnerships without borders, make decisions based on evidence for accountability, and broaden definitions of the campus itself.

As a follow up to *Envisioning the Future of Student Affairs* (Task Force, 2010), Task Force members Kent Porterfield, Larry Roper, and Elizabeth

Whitt (2011) offered some additional ideas about how to "redefine" student affairs work. They suggested that redefining student affairs work might require new structures with fewer, rather than more, specialties and boundaries, and argued that reorganizing some aspects of student affairs practice might be necessary to achieve specific educational outcomes and institutional objectives. They also suggested that this rethinking might require the development of different organizational structures or models that could serve more students, and more diverse students, more effectively. In addition, they argued that student affairs should focus on institutional success, rather than preservation of turf and boundaries. Rethinking, they said, need not require a departure from the field's enduring core values, but should involve constructing broader learning agendas and partnerships that stretch the traditional boundaries of student affairs, with students as our focus, and greater responsibility for leading in new ways to support the success and missions of the institutions.

All of the challenges the ACPA-NASPA Task Force report identified in 2010 are still with us today. We can debate whether any of the Task Force's recommendations have been implemented, but we prefer to focus on the future. That led us and our co-editors to create this sourcebook about trends, opportunities, and challenges for senior student affairs leaders. We started with two questions. First, what are the challenges and opportunities facing student affairs leaders? Second, given what we know about the current state of higher education, how can we help to create a sustainable approach to student affairs leadership in a volatile environment that also continues to focus on creating and sustaining high-quality educational environments and experiences for students?

In the chapters that follow we describe and discuss how student affairs leaders assisted us in answering those two questions. The six themes about "What troubles you?" are described and discussed in Chapter 2 and the six themes about "What keeps you going?" are discussed in Chapter 3. In Chapter 4, we ponder the similarities and differences in the data across the themes and questions and offer some propositions regarding the implications of what we learned from the respondents for current and future student affairs leadership.

## References

American Association for Higher Education (AAHE), American College Personnel Association (ACPA), & National Association of Student Personnel Administrators (NASPA). (1998). *Powerful partnerships: A shared responsibility for learning.* Washington, DC: American College Personnel Association.

American Association of Community Colleges (AACC), American Association of State Colleges and Universities (ASCU), & Association of Public and Land-Grant Universities (APLU). (2015). *Advancing a comprehensive study of post-collegiate outcomes.* Washington, DC: Authors.

American College Personnel Association (ACPA). (1975). A student development model for student affairs in tomorrow's higher education. *Journal of College Student Personnel, 16,* 334–341.

American College Personnel Association (ACPA). (1994). *The student learning imperative: Implications for student affairs.* Washington, DC: Author.

American College Personnel Association (ACPA) & National Association of Student Personnel Administrators (NASPA). (1997). *Principles of good practice for student affairs.* Washington, DC: Authors.

American Council on Education (ACE). (1937). *The student personnel point of view: A report of a conference on the philosophy and development of student personnel work in colleges and universities.* American Council on Education Study, Series 1, Vol. 1, No. 3. Washington, DC: Author.

American Council on Education (ACE). (1949). *The student personnel point of view.* Washington, DC: Author.

Andreas, R. E., & Schuh, J. H. (1999). The student affairs landscape: Focus on learning. In E. J. Whitt (Ed.), *Student learning as student affairs work: Responding to our imperative* (pp. 1–9). Washington, DC: National Association of Student Personnel Administrators.

Appleton, J. R., Briggs, C. M., & Rhatigan, J. J. (1978). *Pieces of eight: The rites, roles, and styles of the dean by eight who have been there.* Portland, OR: National Association of Student Personnel Administrators.

Arum, R., & Roksa, J. (2011). *Academically adrift: Limited learning on college campuses.* Chicago, IL: University of Chicago Press.

Atwell, R. H. (1994). Higher education path to progress. In D. H. Finifer & A. M. Hauptman (Eds.), *America's investment in liberal education* (pp. 125–132). New Directions for Higher Education, No. 85. San Francisco, CA: Jossey-Bass.

Blimling, G. S., Whitt, E. J., & Associates (1999). *Good practice in student affairs: Principles to foster student learning.* San Francisco, CA: Jossey-Bass.

Blumenstyk, G. (2015). *American higher education in crisis? What everyone needs to know.* New York, NY: Oxford University Press.

Boyer Commission on Educating Undergraduates in the Research University. (1998). *Reinventing undergraduate education: A blueprint for America's research universities.* Stony Brook, NY: Author.

Brown, R. D. (1972). *Student development in tomorrow's higher education: A return to the academy.* (Student Personnel Series No. 16). Washington, DC: American College Personnel Association.

Byrne, J. V. (2006). *Public higher education reform five years after the Kellogg Commission on the Future of State and Land-Grant Universities.* Washington, DC: National Association of State Universities and Land-Grant Colleges and W.K. Kellogg Foundation.

Carey, K. (2015). *The end of college: Creating the future of learning and the university of everywhere.* New York, NY: Riverhead.

Craig, R. (2015). *College disrupted: The great unbundling of higher education.* New York, NY: Palgrave Macmillan.

Johnson, C. S., & Cheatham, H. E. (Eds.). (1999). *Higher education trends for the next century: A research agenda for student success.* Washington, DC: American College Personnel Association.

Keeling, R. P., & Hersh, R. H. (2011). *We're losing our minds: Rethinking American higher education.* New York, NY: Palgrave Macmillan.

Kuh, G. D., Whitt, E. J., & Shedd, J. D. (1987). *Student affairs work, 2001: A paradigmatic odyssey.* ACPA Media No. 42. Alexandria, VA: American College Personnel Association.

Lloyd-Jones, E. M. (1954). *Student personnel work as deeper teaching.* New York, NY: Harper.

Lumina Foundation for Education. (2009). *Goal 2025: Lumina Foundation's strategic plan*. Indianapolis, IN: Author.
Mueller, K. H. (1961). *Student personnel work in higher education*. New York, NY: Houghton Mifflin.
National Association of State Universities and Land-Grant Colleges (NASULGC). (1997). *Returning to our roots: The student experience*. Washington, DC: Author.
National Association of State Universities and Land-Grant Colleges (NASULGC). (1999). *Returning to our roots: A learning society*. Washington, DC: Author.
National Association of State Universities and Land-Grant Colleges (NASULGC). (2000). *Returning to our roots: Toward a coherent campus culture*. Washington, DC: Author.
National Association of Student Personnel Administrators (NASPA) & American College Personnel Association (ACPA). (2004). *Learning reconsidered: A campus-wide focus on the student experience*. Washington, DC: Authors.
Porterfield, K. T., Roper, L. D., & Whitt, E. J. (2011). Redefining our mission: What does higher education need from student affairs? *Journal of College & Character, 12*(4), 1–7.
Shapiro, H. (2005). *A larger sense of purpose: Higher education and society*. Princeton, NJ: Princeton University Press.
Shirky, C. (2014, January 29). The end of higher education's golden age [Weblog post]. Retrieved from http://www.shirky.com/weblog/2014/01/there-isnt-enough-money-to-keep-educating-adults-the-way-were-doing-it/
Study Group on the Conditions of Excellence in American Higher Education (Study Group). (1984). *Involvement in learning: Realizing the potential of American higher education: Final report*. Washington, DC: National Institute of Education.
Task Force on the Future of Student Affairs (Task Force). (2010). *Envisioning the future of student affairs: Final report of the task force on the future of student affairs*. Washington, DC: ACPA & NASPA.
U.S. Department of Education. (2006). *A test of leadership: Charting the future of U.S. higher education*. Washington, DC: Author.
White House. (2013). *The President's plan to make college more affordable: A better bargain for the middle class. Fact Sheet*. Washington, DC: Author.

KENT T. PORTERFIELD *is vice president for student development at Saint Louis University.*

ELIZABETH J. WHITT *is vice provost and dean for undergraduate education and professor in sociology at University of California, Merced.*

2

*Responses of student affairs leaders to questions about the challenges and obstacles they find in their work are examined and discussed.*

# What Troubles You? What Keeps You up at Night?

*Larry D. Roper, Elizabeth J. Whitt*

> [What troubles me is the] increasing complexity of "old issues" ... we have not made great strides in addressing old problems like substance abuse, sexual misconduct, campus civility issues, or the achievement gap. Today, the problems seem more multifaceted and layered. (Respondent 9)

The student affairs leaders who responded to our request for information about their experiences offered many examples of the ways in which their roles are complicated and challenging. Among these challenges, described and examined in this chapter, are insufficient resources, increased scrutiny on institutions, increased litigiousness, the burden of state and federal mandates, mounting tensions related to diversity, and intensity and complexity of students' needs and expectations.

In this chapter, we look at what troubled our respondents with regard to the themes of (a) affordability and access, (b) student health and well-being, (c) diversity and inclusion, (d) regulations and compliance, (e) technology and media, and (f) student affairs leadership. Throughout the chapter, we use the words of respondents to illustrate challenges related to these six themes.

Although we address these themes as though they are discrete, it is likely they interact with one another to shape the student affairs leaders' experiences and to describe them as troubling. That is, the whole probably is greater than the sum of the parts. For example, student success is likely to be influenced by physical and mental health, institutional climates for diversity and inclusion, and use of digital technologies, to mention only a few of the myriad of challenges that could plague a student. Our respondents described the impact that increasing demands for compliance with regulatory mandates have on their ability to attend to other issues, such as student success, student well-being, and other aspects of their roles as campus leaders.

In addition, most of the responses to "What troubles you?" were framed by concerns about resources; these issues were troubling, *in part*, because of limited and declining financial and human resources. Therefore, instead of treating resources as a separate theme, we have discussed it throughout this chapter as a critical context for what troubles the respondents.

## Affordability and Access

### Affordability

> [I am troubled] that we are rapidly escalating the costs of higher education but have not developed ways to critically self-reflect, self-monitor or hold ourselves accountable for responsible investment of tuition and other funding to respond to prioritized student needs; i.e., it continues to cost more to deliver the same instruction and student services without demonstrated value-added. (Respondent 37)

As we noted in Chapter 1, higher education affordability has generated significant, and increasing, legislative energy, media attention, campus conversation, and public dialogue for several decades. Concerns about affordability generally focus on the cost of education, student debt, return on investment, and whether the cost of education is justifiable based on the jobs graduates attain, or the number of students who leave college with significant debt and without a degree. The picture painted by the student affairs leaders suggests the great challenges of leading and managing a conversation that has importance with regard to institutional reputation, institutional survival, student expectations, constituent relationships, and personal and institutional accountability.

Many institutions are tuition driven; student enrollment is their lifeline to survival. Unfortunately, some colleges and universities are struggling with declining enrollments that threaten their capacity to continue operating. Because of tuition dependency of many colleges and universities, when enrollments decline, so too do the resources available to fund staff, programs, and services. The student affairs leaders at small private institutions, in particular, worried about the impact of declining enrollments and the threat fewer students pose to their ability to keep their doors open.

The responses of the student affairs leaders demonstrate a dilemma, one that likely faces many institutional leaders. On one hand, these leaders seem to express the need to sustain tuition at a level that will preserve institutional survival. On the other hand, they express concerns that the cost of attendance presents a significant obstacle to the admission and retention of the most needy students. The student affairs leaders present themselves as advocates to promote access for students from a wide range of backgrounds, as well as provide a quality experience for all students; however, there was frustration at their inability to influence the cost of attendance sufficiently.

External funding also influences the cost of attendance at colleges and universities, which includes state appropriations to public institutions, external financial aid for which students might be eligible, and resources received from other funders in the form of donations and grants. The aggregate of funds received directly influences the levels at which institutions are able to operate. In too many cases, institutions are faced with a complex picture of declining or stable enrollments, declining resources, and increasing costs. The student affairs leaders articulated the challenges posed for every aspect of their work by resource constraints, including their commitment to affordability and access to ensuring success for students.

In addition, there was concern that the push for greater affordability might have a negative impact on the capacity of institutions to focus holistically on student learning and educational quality. All too quickly in times of financial constraints, the first impulse is to hunker down to preserve what a unit or division has rather than look outward for ways to collaborate and maintain the focus on holistic learning. Among the challenges related to affordability were increasing calls for on-line education and services, as well as emphases on badges, certificates, and other means of stacking credentials and competencies to prepare students for jobs.

### Access to Success

> The attainment gap issues that result in low completion rates for low-income [students], first-generation [students], and students of color are a national disgrace. I see this as the most compelling issue of our time and think we are generally unprepared for the waves of new students coming to our campuses in the next 10 years ... All in a time of constrained resources (Respondent 19)

Calls for affordability are, in many cases, based on concern about access to higher education for students from groups historically underrepresented in higher education (e.g., first-generation students, low-income students, students of color). And, although they acknowledge and praise the increasing diversity of students on their campuses, the student affairs leaders also emphasized that access to enrollment is not access to success, including academic retention, achievement, and persistence to graduation. Thus, conversations about affordability and access are incomplete if they do not include discussion about—and specific commitments to—what is needed to retain and ensure students' success.

Our respondents questioned the extent to which their institutions are prepared to meet their responsibilities to increasingly diverse student populations. Some of our respondents specifically mentioned the failure of American colleges and universities to attract, retain, and facilitate the success of Black students.

However, the student affairs leaders expressed a desire to help their institutions respond to the disturbing and widening achievement gap between historically underrepresented students and their more affluent peers. Students' zip codes often portray a telling tale of past access to lower quality schools, lack of support, fewer co-curricular options, and the potential for future success at institutions of higher education. Our respondents seek a prominent role in constructing their institutions' approaches to attracting and supporting the diverse students to whom colleges and universities are providing access.

**Summary.** Concerns about the cost of attendance at colleges and universities are shared by the student affairs leaders. Comments about affordability and access also revealed the challenges leaders face in balancing commitments to institutional survival, increasing access for students historically underrepresented in higher education, and supporting the educational success of all students.

## Student Health and Well-Being

> Issues of campus safety and student well-being are a concern for me. Gun issues are a real threat, and particularly when coupled with the trend of mental health challenges that today's college students are presenting in increasingly larger numbers. And even at [my institution], with a relatively "well off" student demographic, we are seeing more homelessness, hunger, and financial crises than previously. (Respondent 9)

Our respondents cited a wide range of concerns regarding the well-being of students, as well as the attention and support required to address those concerns effectively, including mental health and wellness, violence and campus and student safety; and, in general, the enormity of challenges some students face in their quest for higher education.

### Mental Health and Wellness

> Many of our students carry heavy individual burdens that affect their behaviors and performance on a university campus. How do we weigh their personal situations vs. the needs of other students on campus? None of us ever knows when everything might need to be dropped to work on a student or campus emergency. (Respondent 10)

The student affairs leaders offered many comments about the perceived fragility of contemporary college students, including declining resilience and escalating mental health issues. Statements suggested that current college students are more fragile and less resilient in facing the ups and downs of daily life than was the case for previous generations of students. As a result, they require more time and resources and a different kind of attention from student affairs staff. These comments also echoed messages in the popular media questioning whether today's students possess the necessary fortitude and resiliency to navigate the social and campus experiences with which they are confronted (Gray, 2015). Student mental health—that is, the volume and complexity of serious student mental health issues—also was cited frequently as troubling to our respondents. Postsecondary institutions are confronted with the responsibility to serve increasing numbers of students requiring mental health support and/or intervention. The student affairs leaders' perspectives reflect those found in the mainstream media (Henriques, 2014) and in comprehensive surveys of college and university counseling centers (see Mistler, Reetz, Krylowicz, & Barr, 2012). The sheer volume of student mental health issues is made more taxing by the number of serious cases that involve more than a relationship between an individual student and a therapist, cases that require intervention, the deployment of crisis or care teams, and that may require balancing student conduct processes with accommodations for disabilities.

## Campus and Student Safety

> ... what keeps me awake is safety ... I don't feel that I can assure parents that their sons/daughters will be safe in college. I feel that as institutions we are doing more than ever to educate them about risks and reduce violence but it is still a major challenge. These risks have always been present; the degree just seems higher to me now. (Respondent 32)

General and specific concerns about campus and student safety were troubling to many of our respondents. And, although the student affairs leaders consistently communicated their commitment to serving students, concern for protecting students from violence implied a more intense level of concern. This probably was related to the timing of our request for assistance; our e-mail message went out in the midst of a spate of violent incidents on campuses across the United States.

Although the student affairs leaders expressed trepidation about some safety issues, their comments regarding the fear of gun violence seemed to reflect a much deeper emotion. The fact that some respondents work on campuses that have experienced gun violence and most have colleagues, family, or friends on campuses that have been touched by gun-related campus tragedies could add to the fear that gun violence on campuses is no longer an unlikely occurrence. Our respondents expressed helplessness that random acts of crime are being perpetrated against students and other campus community members.

Concern for protecting campuses from gun violence is further complicated by the unfortunate connection that can be made between mental health and violence (Saad, 2013). The student affairs leaders presented the breadth and depth of this challenge by positioning the need to address the profound and serious mental health issues facing campuses *and* protecting students from random acts of violence as significant issues of campus health and well-being. At the center of this challenge is the obligation to serve mental health needs responsibly without stigmatizing those receiving mental health services in the process. In this regard, the student affairs leaders identified the increased need to engage in threat assessment of students as a way of determining when or if an individual poses a risk to the campus.

### Implications of Health and Safety Concerns for Campus Resources

> [I am troubled] that growing pressures to become social welfare agencies (responding to mental health issues, sexual violence/sexual misconduct, etc.) draws personnel, fiscal, and time resources away from our educational and learning missions—an ethical dilemma that is challenging to resolve. (Respondent 37)

The student affairs leaders were committed to the access and success of the most needy students in our society. At the same time, the growing number of students manifesting multifaceted and multilayered life situations not only indicates heavy individual burdens that affect the students' behaviors and performance on campus, but also creates a heavy load for student affairs organizations. As our respondents noted, they are called upon to deal with student homelessness, hunger, mental illness, and financial crises. The increase in student manifestation of needs that traditionally have been addressed by social service agencies is requiring some colleges and universities to implement services and programs outside of the areas of conventional student affairs preparation. The commitment of new resources to the human service needs of students poses a dilemma for leaders: How do organizations meet both the extreme personal situations facing students and the needs of other students on campus in a climate of shrinking resources?

**Summary.** Attending to issues of student health and well-being requires student affairs leaders to provide leadership for a wide range of difficult situations, ranging from matters of food insecurity to the unpredictability of gun violence. Some of these issues fall within the realm of areas in which student affairs professionals might have received professional preparation, and others are emerging issues that require the cultivation of new skills and increased awareness as well as partnering with other agencies beyond an institution's borders. In all cases, student affairs leadership appears essential to ensure institutional awareness, readiness, and response. Why? Student affairs leadership and departments often play the role of generalists and boundary spanners within institutions, and these skills and relationships across departments are critical to meet the needs of student and campus safety.

## Diversity and Inclusion

> What troubles me are all of the persons underrepresented in higher education who will experience few, if any, of the perks of the "American Dream" during a lifetime. Our world suffers, therefore. (Respondent 27)

Current conversations regarding institutional leadership for diversity and inclusion take place under urgent conditions that present campus leaders with significant challenges, challenges noted by most of our respondents. Student affairs leaders expressed a range of concerns on this topic, but they focused primarily on the lack of institutional readiness to address the diverse and complex identities, needs, and demands presented by today's students.

### More Diversity Doesn't Necessarily Mean Greater Inclusion

> [What troubles me is the] pervasive alienation and hostility that continue to taint the experiences of students, staff, and faculty with nondominant and marginalized identities. (Respondent 4)

While acknowledging and celebrating increasing student diversity on their campuses, the student affairs leaders also expressed frustration about the presence of gender, racial, and other social identity inequities in a milieu (i.e., higher education) that professes otherwise. That is, leaders in higher education and on campuses express commitment to diversity, while continuing to function in ways that perpetuate inequality, as well as demonstrating little understanding of the dimensions of diversity among students. Comments from our respondents included distaste for reductionistic descriptions of students (e.g., millenials, entitled, unprepared, lacking resilience) and their backgrounds that ignore differences and complexities that must be recognized and understood to serve students effectively. Such general characterizations disregard—among other things—the ethnic, racial, gender, cultural, and socioeconomic diversity of students on every campus, thereby distorting the truths of individual students' identities and experiences. They can also reinforce institutional structures, cultures, and practices in ways that create barriers to student success and diminish student talent and agency.

These and other factors have influenced colleges and universities to develop cultures that do not always effectively address the diverse identities, lifestyles, needs, expectations, and realities of today's college students. The student protests and activism colleges and universities are experiencing today grow out of specific incidents on some campuses, but also out of mounting general frustration with the failure of campuses to even acknowledge, let alone achieve, diversity and inclusion at a level acceptable to students. Colleges and universities are under pressure to address the needs of increasingly diverse student bodies in ways that students will accept as meaningful and appropriate. Students are protesting institutions' failure to live up to their implied promise to provide students with the campus environments that accord them a sense of place and show regard for their identities (Griggs, 2015; Hartocollis, 2015; Loughlin, 2015).

**Institutional and Student Affairs Responses to Diversity**

> As our campuses become increasingly more diverse in every way, I worry that our current models of practice were designed for another time. Developing models of practice (and even organizational structures) for homogeneous student populations is much easier than designing approaches for increasingly heterogeneous populations ... Students' needs seem to be increasingly more individualistic (think intersectionality). I believe this requires a different approach, and I do worry about whether we have the stomach for this type of dramatic shift in our field. (Respondent 9)

The student affairs leaders worried about the ability of their institutions to live up to the values of diversity and inclusion they espouse. Lack of knowledge and skills—even will—on the part of leaders about how to create inclusive communities, and lack of diversity in faculty and staff hiring, can produce superficial and unsustainable responses to concerns about developing and maintaining effective campus climates for diverse students, faculty, and staff.

The student affairs leaders also suggested that student affairs organizations are carrying out institutions' diversity and social justice missions and values without much support or similar efforts from other parts of the campus. Our respondents perceived that they are carrying a heavier responsibility regarding diversity and inclusion than other institutional leaders. For example, they reported engaging in difficult tasks of managing diversity-related campus disruptions, helping campuses to reconcile the tension between commitments to freedom of expression and student learning, and the press to address microaggressions and psychological triggers.

At the same time, some expressed reservations about whether student affairs units are, in fact, organized effectively to address the educational and inclusion needs of all students, especially those who are not first-time, full time, residential students.

**Summary.** The student affairs leaders found myriad challenges to diversity and inclusion on their campuses. Many commented that they and their staffs, more than other institutional entities, have responsibility for creating and sustaining inclusive communities and responding to challenges to inclusion. At the same time, some of our respondents wondered if today's student affairs organizations are organized and are up to managing all these tasks effectively, a topic to which we will return to later in this chapter.

## Regulations and Compliance

> The governmental activism—from many different fronts—is frantic and has become unnecessarily intrusive into our work. We need to find an appropriate balance between the urgent need to focus on these issues, and the ability for institutions to develop and manage their own processes, policies, programs, and services. (Respondent 52)

## Burdens of Compliance

> [I am troubled by] the increasing administrative and compliance burdens generated by state and federal legislatures, as well as external regulatory entities such as accreditation bodies, are diverting us away from transformational leadership by keeping us occupied with management of transactional tasks. (Respondent 37)

American postsecondary institutions are subject to increasing demands for compliance with federal regulations. This regulatory activity has steadily increased during the past decade and has gained even more intensity the last 3 years (Task Force on Federal Regulation of Higher Education, 2013). In addition, public colleges and universities have seen greater involvement by state-level entities in shaping institutional policies, practices, and reporting. It should come as no surprise that most of our respondents expressed concerns and frustrations about the breadth and weight of external mandates and the resources required to comply with them.

Although compliance with governmental mandates represented a significant burden to the student affairs leaders, they also cited other related factors as troubling. Those factors included the current, and largely negative, public discourse about the value of higher education; the perceived conflicts between regulations and compliance and student learning; and the burden of responding to external expectations at the same time institutional resources for core functions have declined (see *The Cost of Federal Regulatory Compliance at Colleges and Universities: A Multi-Institutional Study*, 2015). Indeed, the focus of a number of responses was the troubling amount of time, energy, and resources consumed by compliance-related activities that could not, therefore, be spent on activities related to student learning and student health and well-being.

Student affairs leaders worry about the risks associated with leading their organizations in this regulatory climate. With responsibility comes fear of falling short on major compliance issues and the consequences of doing so, consequences that can include fines, harm to institutional reputations, damage to personal reputations, and risks to one's professional viability. In addition, they noted the financial costs of compliance, including responding to reporting requirements, and the inability—as institutional resources shrink—to add staff positions or expand staff responsibilities to accommodate new mandates; this exacerbates concern about the risks of responding inadequately to compliance demands. Our respondents acknowledged the critical importance of campus safety and the necessity of responding effectively to all forms of violence, but they believed the federal and state mandates constitute a continual and evolving challenge but do not necessarily address the growing safety issues.

The student affairs leaders also noted the relationship between calls for regulation and compliance and the current public discourse on higher education, and they were troubled by the lack of public trust in and support for higher education. State and federal officials were perceived as politicizing educational institutions and, in the process, undermining the effectiveness of colleges and universities and diminishing awareness of the public good institutions provide. The creation of state and federal metrics in the form of "dashboards" create the feeling that government leaders are attempting to satisfy the public by trying to guarantee outcomes. These measures created fear that institutions are being homogenized and that government officials lack awareness of the distinctions among institutions in different sectors of higher education (e.g., 2-year, 4-year, public, private, etc.).

### Title IX, in Particular

> It's not that I am reluctant to take on high expectations for our response to sexual harassment/assault; it's that the DOE OCR [Department of Education] [Office of Civil Rights] has dictated so many aspects of how we respond ... our Title IX process is becoming less and less an educational process and more of a legal/criminal one. The saddest part is that these are situations in which students need our expertise the most, and we are increasingly denied the opportunity to do what we do best. (Respondent 35)

The weight of Title IX was the compliance challenge identified most frequently by the student affairs leaders. Adding to the complexity and risks in dealing with already very difficult situations is media attention that can lead to publicity and public criticism, no matter what actions are, or are not, taken. Although the student affairs leaders were clear in their commitment to addressing issues of sexual violence, regulations and policies were viewed as inadequate responses to these issues. Instead, they advocated for better prevention and education strategies as means to achieve lasting behavioral and cultural change regarding sexual violence. They contended that the response protocols called for do very little to help in this regard and, instead, encourage reactive approaches to incidents for which campuses would prefer to be more proactive.

**Summary.** The student affairs leaders suggested that the proliferation of regulatory requirements, combined with the complexity and intensity of attention to matters of student conduct—especially sexual assault—create pressure to focus on legal, rather than educational, matters. They also described feeling a need to be reactive, rather than purposeful, and to focus more on compliance than on care. Our respondents expressed a strong desire to protect students from harm, but they also expressed doubt that current compliance protocols and other requirements actually are helpful in creating safer campus environments for learning.

## Technology and Media

> I worry that technology, no matter how sophisticated, will not replace a caring faculty or staff member who advocates on behalf of a student (thousands of them across the country on any given day) and turns a disappointment into an opportunity to excel. (Respondent 6)

The student affairs leaders reported that contending with the rapid growth of technology, students' heavy use of and reliance on digital technologies and social media, and the urgency and instant gratification created by constant access to technology are of major concern to them. Our respondents suggested that the rapid pace of advances in technology and their inability to keep up in terms of training and adoption of new practices is a challenge, and can further disadvantage first-generation students or those who have limited finances.

### Impact of Technologies on Student Affairs Work

> The 24-hour news cycle and the reality of nonstop social media has not only changed how students interact, but has also changed the way activism happens on our campuses and in society. Things move at warp speed today, offering student affairs professionals and other campus officials very little time to think and respond. (Respondent 9)

The impact of digital technologies and the use of social media on the pace, and, in some cases, the nature of student affairs work was a consistent thread through the student affairs leaders' responses. They noted that the 24-hr news/social media cycle can result in misleading and reckless information being widely disseminated, thereby affecting the speed with which campuses must respond to crises and amid external distractions to sensitive internal procedures. There is concern that the issues covered through social media by traditional and web-based news agencies are not always managed responsibly by those doing the reporting, and social media platforms are not appropriate or effective media for messaging complex issues. Instantaneous reporting of news bites and instantaneous responses on Twitter, for example, can create even more problems for a campus already dealing with a crisis.

Our respondents also questioned whether instructional and service technologies would ever be able to mediate interactions with students at such a level as to reliably and effectively influence such factors as community, student engagement, and intentional learning. Although acknowledging the vast potential technology has for improving student affairs work, doubts were expressed that any electronic devices, applications, or programs can substitute for in-person interactions with faculty and staff members who care about students.

The student affairs leaders drew a connection between their ability to use certain technologies and their ability to stay current, meaning they felt the need to be aware of current technological innovations and, therefore, the need to have the capacity to utilize those tools to serve students effectively. Keeping in touch with students and making sure they receive—let alone read—necessary information (from advising deadlines, to campus activities, to emergency alerts) in a timely fashion is increasingly challenging as students' attention shifts from e-mail to Facebook to Twitter to Instagram and so on.

Nevertheless, ability to keep up with technology is influenced by the financial and human resources available to invest in the necessary systems and/or equipment and update them regularly. Thus, the student affairs leaders wrestled with appropriate ways to incorporate technology, finding the necessary resources to invest, and finding the time to engage in the appropriate training to keep up to date.

The student affairs leaders' views on technology and social media were, however, contradictory. On one hand, the technologies were viewed as an enhancement to student learning and service delivery (more on this topic in Chapter 3). On the other hand, the technologies, especially social media, were seen as increasing the impact of campus events and adding urgency to respond to those events even beyond the campus.

### Students and Digital Technologies

> I worry that we have forgotten how to have face-to-face conversations. When students need to talk it out with their peers—they don't know how. That inability to seek support or advice or feedback leaves people isolated or ill informed. (Respondent 51)

In addition to grappling with their own use of technology, the student affairs leaders found students' use of digital technologies, especially social media, challenging. The mainstream media have covered the prominence of technology use among college students (Smith, Rainie, & Zickuhr, 2011). Those reports reinforce the experiences of the student affairs leaders who express concern that having 24 hour access to communication devices and social media platforms has dramatically changed student communications and communities, and not always for the better. For example, they viewed student use of digital technologies as impeding interaction and personal connection.

In addition, the devices and social media have affected the climates and experiences student affairs professionals often are expected to monitor and shape, and in which they also are expected to participate. The student affairs leaders are challenged to monitor social media for social trends, to stay abreast of on- and off-campus activities, and to be aware of possible student behavior issues. Student affairs leaders also must address issues of student misuse of technology, particularly via social media sites that allow for bullying, intimidation, dehumanizing activity, and other behaviors that create hostile situations for students. Our respondents expressed concern about the potential recklessness of students' use of social media and the ways in which social media can work against campus expectations for fostering community and human dignity.

Our respondents specifically cited the relationship among student activism, social media, and news agency coverage as an issue that troubles them. Student activists increasingly use social media to create awareness of their causes and to engage allies (Loughlin, 2015). Meanwhile, news agencies use their own online presence to offer coverage and commentary of those campus incidents. When this coverage is inaccurate or does not fairly represent what occurs, it not only influences perceptions on and off campus but also changes how students interact and the way subsequent activism happens.

**Summary.** The student affairs leaders view digital technologies as tools to enhance student learning and success, and recognized social media play a prominent role in the lives of most students. However, our respondents worried about their ability to keep pace with technological innovations, in terms of the financial and human resources needed. Social media have become an important vehicle for student affairs organizations as they attempt to stay in touch with students, student issues, social trends, student attitudes and behaviors, and the ability to communicate effectively with students. Our respondents also commented on the challenges they face in dealing with the impacts of misuse of social media by students, news agencies, and others. Social media add to the complexity and intensity of student affairs work by creating climates of crisis, urgency, and instant gratification. This outcome requires student affairs presence and engagement not just in the physical environment of the campus but also in virtual environments.

## Student Affairs Leadership

> The lack of awareness about how students learn and develop among student affairs professionals and the academy as a whole keeps me awake at night. To cite the wisdom of the *Student Learning Imperative*, student learning and development are inextricably intertwined ... If student affairs professionals in particular don't begin to rethink the way they do their work and evaluate it—who exactly will be [invited to] the table about what the commodity of higher education actually is? (Respondent 42)

In the previous sections of this chapter, we described a number of challenges experienced by our respondents. For many, challenges are further complicated by their struggles to clarify and/or affirm their own identity and the identity of their organizations within the academy. In this section, we explore aspects of the concerns about student affairs leadership expressed by our respondents. The student affairs leaders appeared to be wrestling with an uneasiness about their status in the academy, recognition of student affairs contributions, and how to navigate the discordant responsibilities assigned to student affairs organizations successfully.

### A Role and Voice for Student Affairs

> My concern is that [student] affairs is not sufficiently involved in issues of educational quality, student success, and the broader spectrum of student learning outcomes on most campuses. As we know, student affairs educators have a lot to contribute, but they don't seem to have found their way into relevant conversations if this is happening on campuses, or aren't in good positions to lead the discussion if others aren't taking them up on campus. (Respondent 20)

As institutions respond to growing public concerns and media discourse about the value of and need for higher education, and as governments and funding agencies produce their versions of effectiveness, the student affairs leaders worried about their ability to demonstrate value and relevance, as well as engage in the campus conversations that matter most for institutional and student success. Our respondents also questioned whether student affairs leaders have effectively constructed an evidenced-based narrative that is compelling to those who are making judgments about what constitutes success at colleges and universities. In addition, although they noted that student affairs has much to contribute to institutional and student success, our respondents perceived that student affairs leaders and their organizations have not been sufficiently articulate or assertive about these contributions.

Our respondents expressed concerns that, because student affairs professionals are absent from important conversations, evidence of the value of student affairs work is also absent in local, national, and state-level reports on factors related to student and institutional success. Thus, lack of involvement in important conversations—whether through lack of attention to the content and strategic necessity of those conversations or through exclusion from them by other institutional leaders—perpetuates itself to further obscure the voices of student affairs leadership.

In addition, concerns were expressed that the leading student affairs professional associations have not been as successful as they might be in advocating for the presence of student affairs points of view and contributions in arenas where public policy decisions are made. The implication is that effective representation by professional associations would bring attention to student affairs contributions to student learning (e.g., leadership, cultural competencies) and the role student affairs plays in promoting student success (e.g., fulfilling institutions' completion agendas). The student affairs leaders expressed a desire to have a voice in the policy conversations that affect their work lives and to be respected for the quality work they do on behalf of colleges and universities. Finding such a voice might require student affairs leaders to become more multilingual—to speak in the voice of the educator whose core work addresses the range of needs students bring to the college or university experience, as well as the voice of an institutional leader who understands and responds effectively to all of the institution's internal and external priorities.

### Evidence of Effectiveness

> I worry that we are still struggling to codify, capture, and articulate the powerful learning that occurs outside the classroom in conversations about the value of college. (Respondent 6)

Concerns about relevance and centrality of student affairs were also reflected in comments from the respondents about data and evidence. Some noted that student affairs, as a field and on campuses, still appears to be struggling to capture and represent the powerful learning that occurs outside the classroom appropriately and to have those data included in the institutional and national discourse on the value of higher education. The absence of those data and the student affairs voice puts student affairs professionals in the position of fearing that their relevance and necessity will be questioned as the future of higher education is being defined.

This concern echoes a consistent theme in the culture of many student affairs organizations and for many student affairs professionals: fears about relevance, feelings of being marginalized citizens in the academy, and unease about the value that others have for work performed by student affairs professionals. Student affairs leaders are now confronted with the task of demonstrating clearly their essential contributions to the future success of their institutions and higher education by producing the evidence necessary to demonstrate effectiveness in achieving desired institutional outcomes. Such outcomes will require acquiring new language to participate in institutional and public discourse, understanding the evolving frame through which higher education is being evaluated, and developing new approaches to making meaning of student affairs outcomes.

### Organizational Models

> How do we re-engineer, reorganize, merge, and cut to realize efficiencies? I have a thought about this ... the idea that the age of specialization may and

> should come to an end in student affairs. We have seen significant specialization over the past 25 years, more services, more experts, more departments. I wonder if we need to begin thinking about a return to more generalists—student affairs staff that have broader sets of responsibilities. (Respondent 19)

As noted earlier in this chapter, some of our respondents raised questions about the current state of student affairs organizations on their campuses and whether those units are structured to respond to rapid student and institutional change amid declining resources. Concerns were expressed about overspecialization, as expressed in the quotation above. That is, do more specialties within student affairs organizations necessarily serve an increasingly diverse student body more effectively? Or, does more specialization mean more duplication of effort, which is good for neither students nor institutions, and creates still greater segmentation of students' lives? The need for seamless living and learning environments for students was also reflected in respondent unease about traditional structures—"silos"—of academic and student affairs, which might also serve to limit student affairs involvement in the academic mission of the institution.

Some student affairs leaders also noted the advantages and disadvantages to student affairs of new models of effectiveness, including, for example, "corporatization of college" (Blumenstyk, 2015, p. 121). To some, this perspective is seen as antithetical to the educational relationships that are student affairs work; there is concern that viewing the goals of higher education through a business frame reduces education to transactions. On the other hand, some respondents see business models of effectiveness in the light of a press for greater accountability and see an emphasis on concrete outcomes, such as graduation rates and cost of degrees awarded as meaningful measures of institutional—and student affairs—effectiveness. Perhaps the challenge before student affairs is to operate successfully by honoring both perspectives, that higher education is an experience of personal educational relationships, and higher education operates and is evaluated by business principles that require the presentation of concrete, measurable outcomes.

### Professional Performance and Identity

> Student affairs does not have a clear and understandable narrative. We do not connect our work directly to recruitment/enrollment, persistence/retention [or] completion ... We do not tell our stories well. We have not been effective in creating a compelling evidence-based narrative. (Respondent 1)

The day-to-day life of senior student affairs leaders has grown more complex, evolving to include a range of disparate and sometimes conflicting roles, including student support and engagement, enrollment management, crisis and risk management, athletics, fundraising, financial administration, regulatory compliance, external communications, and supervision of a wide range of units and staff expertise. This array of activities suggests increased expectations of student affairs leaders and their organizations, as well as the need for a wider range of expertise and knowledge than, perhaps, has been required in the past.

The disparate, even conflicting, nature of responsibilities was reflected in respondents' statements about the difficulty they face in balancing the roles they have as educators with the increasing demand that they perform as crisis managers. This tension has emerged because of the growing number of high-need students enrollment, the increased incidents of distressed and disruptive behavior, and the high stakes associated with addressing Title IX, and other potentially litigious situations. As a result, some senior student affairs leaders find themselves performing roles inconsistent with the career for which they were prepared as well as the expectations, knowledge, and skill set they brought to the role. Thus, many leaders find themselves needing to commit more time and resources to hone their skills as crisis managers, development officers, institutional strategic planners, and accountants, and they are having to reconsider their professional identities in light of the emergent realities of their role.

Consistent with the concern about professional identities was concern about professional preparation. A perceived decline in interest in professional preparation and experience in student affairs—or, even, in higher education—as a qualification for contemporary student affairs leaders was raised as a concern in our respondents' responses. Such a decline could suggest that traditional student affairs education and pathways to student affairs leadership are inadequate in light of contemporary demands. Or, it could suggest that a sufficient case has not been made for the value of such preparation for institutional leadership. Apprehension about the perceived value of student affairs preparation and experience is consistent with concerns about general recognition of student affairs contributions and full engagement of student affairs leaders in achieving broad institutional goals.

Indeed, some respondents questioned whether it is prudent to continue to educate student affairs professionals in traditional ways—with traditional curricula and experiences—when it is so clear that student populations and institutional expectations are rapidly changing. A related concern was whether the student affairs profession is attracting individuals with the greatest potential for leadership to its preparation programs and whether those who are entering the profession have the necessary resilience and bandwidth to be successful over time.

**Summary.** Senior student affairs leaders seek to bring coherence, balance and value to their leadership roles. In the current climate, for some the role appears to have become muddled, uneven, and underappreciated. Leaders desire to gain a prominent voice for themselves, recognition of the essential contributions of student affairs organizations, and acknowledgment of the unique skills and background necessary to perform the student affairs role. They want to carve out space for themselves to participate in and contribute to the institutional accountability and effectiveness, as well as gain acknowledgment of student affairs outcomes in national reports on higher education success. Embedded in the student affairs leaders' responses to what they find troubling was a consistent message of the need to assert articulately and convincingly the significance of student affairs as a profession, to demonstrate the specific contributions of student affairs programs, strengthen the quality of student affairs leadership, and to claim space for student affairs as full partners in the work of the academy.

## Conclusion

The student affairs leaders responded to the query of "What keeps you up at night?" by offering descriptions of a leadership role that has become increasingly weighty and complex. Powerful social forces, including politics, poverty, the "isms," mental health, violence and technology, are shaping and reshaping student affairs leadership roles. Leaders are challenged to reconcile the contemporary responsibilities and expectations of their roles with what has been traditionally expected. The responses to this survey question suggest that student affairs administrators are presented with an awesome challenge of finding effective ways to organize and pursue their work in a climate where many are functioning with insufficient resources and inadequate institutional understanding and support.

Student affairs leaders' responses leave little doubt that the need for student affairs leadership in the current higher education environment is significant. What is not yet clear is what approaches, perspectives, models, and organizations will best serve higher education and student affairs in responding to that need. We return to this issue in Chapter 4.

## References

Blumenstyk, G. (2015). *American higher education in crisis? What everyone needs to know*. New York, NY: Oxford University Press.

Gray, P. (2015, September 22). Declining student resilience: A serious problem for colleges. *Psychology Today*. Retrieved from https://www.psychologytoday.com/blog/freedom-learn/201509/declining-student-resilience-serious-problem-colleges

Griggs, B. (2015, November 10). Do U.S. colleges have a race problem? Retrieved from http://www.cnn.com/2015/11/10/us/racism-college-campuses-protests-missouri/

Hartocollis, A. (2015, November 11). Racial discrimination protests ignite at colleges across the U.S. *The New York Times*.

Henriques, G. (2014, February 15). The college student mental health crisis. *Psychology Today*. Retrieved from https://www.psychologytoday.com/blog/theory-knowledge/201402/the-college-student-mental-health-crisis

Loughlin, S. (2015, November 14). A new age of campus activism: Growth of social media, current political climate and desire for change help spur students to speak out.

*Terre Haute Tribune Star.* Retrieved from http://www.tribstar.com/news/local_news/a-new-age-of-campus-activism/article_e550d329-4e39-5f60-a2e9-8b0365d2ae65.html

Mistler, B., Reetz, D., Krylowicz, B., & Barr, V. (2012). *The Association for University and College Counseling Center Directors annual survey.* Retrieved from Association for University and College Counseling Center Directors website: http://files.cmcglobal.com/Monograph_2012_AUCCCD_Public.pdf

Saad, L. (2013, September 20). *Americans fault mental health system most for gun violence.* Retrieved from http://www.gallup.com/poll/164507/americans-fault-mental-health-system-gun-violence.aspx

Smith, A., Rainie, L., & Zickuhr, K. (2011, July 11). *College students and technology.* Retrieved from Pew Research Center website: http://www.pewinternet.org/2011/07/19/college-students-and-technology/

Task Force on Federal Regulation of Higher Education. (2013). *Recalibrating regulation of colleges and universities: Report of the Task Force on Federal Regulation of Higher Education.* Retrieved from American Council on Education website: http://www.acenet.edu/news-room/Documents/Higher-Education-Regulations-Task-Force-Report.pdf

*The cost of federal regulatory compliance at colleges and universities: A multi-institutional study.* (2015). Retrieved from Vanderbilt University website: http://www.nacua.org/documents/costofcompliance.pdf

LARRY D. ROPER *is professor in the School of Language, Culture and Society at Oregon State University and coordinator, College Student Services Administration and Social Justice Minor.*

ELIZABETH J. WHITT *is vice provost and dean for undergraduate education and professor in sociology at University of California, Merced.*

3

*Responses of student affairs leaders to questions about the opportunities and joy they find in their work are examined and discussed.*

# What Excites You? What Keeps You Going?

*Elizabeth J. Whitt, Jill E. Carnaghi*

> Despite the fact that I am sleep deprived, I do what I do because I truly do believe in this work. I am inspired and motivated each and every day by the potential I see in young adults and the role I can play as they immerse themselves in experiences and opportunities that enable them to find, raise, and place their unique voices in the world in ways that are transformative. (Respondent 30)

In Chapter 2, Larry Roper and Elizabeth Whitt examined the issues that troubled and challenged the student affairs leaders who responded to a request to share their experiences. Now we turn our attention to those aspects of their work that excited them, aspects they found inspiring and in which they found joy (both words the respondents used). Perhaps it is not surprising that our respondents had much more to say about what kept them up at night than about what kept them going—65% of the data they provided focused on what was troubling—because we offered them an opportunity to vent for productive purposes. However, the data about what excited them were reassuring and affirming, as the data communicated the meaning and purpose so many student affairs professionals find in their work, as well as the sense of service and serving they find in day-to-day interactions with students, colleagues, campus and community partners, and graduates.

This chapter is organized according to the six themes identified in those data: (a) students, (b) making a difference, (c) collaboration and community, (d) leading and facilitating change, (e) learning, data, and scholarship, and (f) the work. Throughout the chapter, we use the words of respondents to illustrate opportunities related to these six themes.

As in Chapter 2, although we address these themes as though they are discrete, we assume they work together to shape the student affairs leaders' perceptions of what keeps them going. Again, the whole—the experiences of these themes taken together—is greater than the sum of the parts. It is likely, for example, that excitement about student learning is connected to the desire to make a difference in students' lives to collaborating with great colleagues to creating innovative learning opportunities and learning something more in the process. Commitment to diversity and inclusion is most likely inextricably linked to making a difference and facilitating student success. Commitment to making a difference through their work likely weaves seamlessly through our respondents' interest in transforming the composition of the student body and to better serve those who come believing it is a just place for learning. And the joy and fulfillment they feel for the work of student affairs leadership is likely to influence, and be influenced by, all of the other interactions, opportunities, challenges, and experiences that keep them going. Yet, sometimes these joys and inspirations can turn troubling and overly burdensome, and it is a fine line that our respondents walk.

## It's All About the Students

> Interacting with students, hearing about their aspirations and accomplishments, seeing the impacts that they are making on each other, our campus, and our world is truly inspirational. And being able to facilitate this daily is an honor. (Respondent 32)

The student affairs leaders, almost to a person, highlighted or emphasized students as what keeps them going. They described the rewards of interacting with students, as well as facilitating student learning and success through their leadership roles.

### Spending Time with Students and Learning From Students

> [What keeps me going is] direct student engagement. Once a week I carve out a little time just to walk around the [union], which is where our student government, Greek life, and student org offices are located. I take pics with students, just chat with them, and engage. That is better than any cup of coffee. (Respondent 22)

> I'm continually amazed at the resiliency of the human spirit. Every year, I'm astounded when I learn of a student's journey to college. I think "how did they have the resolve to stick with [IT]?" (whatever "it" is). It could be a broken home, personal recovery from alcohol or drug abuse, poverty, mental illness, international travel, world crises, etc. Helping these students achieve their dream of a college education is truly a privilege. (Respondent 3)

Our respondents described the rewards they reaped from spending time with students—"I love working with students," and "Students keep me going" communicate the sense of those descriptions—including being in community with students and seeing themselves as part of opportunities for facilitating student growth that drew them to student affairs work in the first place. And they value spending time with students not only because they enjoy those interactions, but also because of the learning opportunities students provided for the student affairs leaders' own growth and development—professionally and, at times, personally. Our respondents described acting as companions on the students' developmental journeys. For example, the student affairs leaders recounted the inspiration they find in students' stories of resilience, striving, and hunger for education, such as the experiences described in the second quotation above. They also noted the joy they take in being part of the students' college journeys, seeing students learn, develop, and "grow before your eyes" (Respondent 51).

**Facilitating Student Success**

> After 30 plus years in the field I still love my work. Students are by and large fabulous and the opportunity to impact their development, learning, and success is incredibly rewarding and fulfilling. (Respondent 34)

The student affairs leaders also wrote with excitement about helping students learn and succeed. Increasing calls to consider student learning and success as essential measures of institutional effectiveness (see Arum & Roksa, 2011; Blumenstyk, 2015; Keeling & Hersh, 2011; Kuh & Ikenberry, 2009; Kuh, Kinzie, Schuh, Whitt, and associates, 2005, 2010; Lumina Foundation for Education, 2009) were noted and emphasized as positive, offering opportunities for student affairs organizations to be aligned clearly with campus, state, and national priorities of fostering an informed and educated citizenry.

Our respondents expressed their feelings about the centrality of student success to their work with inspiring language, ranging from the personal—observing "the excitement on a student's face when she overcomes an obstacle" (Respondent 10)—to the organizational, including "looking at different options to help students be successful" (Respondent 40) and seeking to "examine our institutional practices, policies, and priorities ... [to] keep the focus ... [on] student success" (Respondent 16). The student affairs leaders have the opportunity to view their work with students both from the person-to-person level of interaction and influence and from an organizational perspective. With the use of those frames, the respondents realized that they could, and did, influence change in very positive and rewarding ways both for students and themselves.

**Summary.** Students are the *raison d'etre* for the work the student affairs leaders are engaged in. As noted previously, our respondents' interactions with students brought them inspiration and learning, and students' success provided a focus for the goals and aspirations not only for themselves but, more importantly, for their organizations.

Stereotypical views of senior student affairs leaders might portray individuals who are far removed, both literally and figuratively, from undergraduate students, but that clearly was not an accurate portrayal of our respondents. This focus on students as central to their efforts, and the reason for those efforts, is consistent with the values and history of student affairs work, which we touched on in Chapter 1 and will return to in Chapter 4.

## Making a Difference

> I love my job. I love the diversity of the challenges and the opportunities to make a real difference in the lives of our students, many of whom are first generation and international. I love "being in charge" in that I can influence a large sector of the institution and the student experience. (Respondent 33)

Again, this respondent readily articulated the "both/and" of the needs of the student and the institution. The ability to make a difference in addressing those issues that was troubling to the respondents was also part of what excited them about their work. As we noted at the beginning of this chapter, the theme of "making a difference" probably is linked inextricably to our respondents' commitment to student success and service with and to others. Within this theme, though, student affairs leaders referred specifically to making a difference because of the power of higher education to change lives and, thereby, to make a difference in the future of the individual student and of the world. In addition, two elements that were seen as troubling also were mentioned as reasons for excitement: challenges posed by increasing campus diversity and increasing use of social media. We look more specifically at the possible intersections and potential relationships between the "What troubles you" data and the "What keeps you going?" data in Chapter 4.

### The Transformative Power of Education

> [What keeps me going] is the continued power of education to transform lives. (Respondent 2)

> What excites me is working in a community college where I am able to serve underrepresented, economically disadvantaged students for whom we can help make the "American Dream" a reality. Our world prospers, therefore. (Respondent 27)

Student affairs leaders referred to the transformative power of education as they described their excitement at making a difference through their work. First-generation students were mentioned specifically as higher education provides them opportunities to change the course of their lives, not only for themselves, but for their families and communities as well. Students' eagerness to give back to their communities through civic engagement was also noted as one of the ways higher education can transform lives on and off campus—well beyond campus borders.

Our respondents also valued the power of higher education to make significant changes in the broader American society, as well as the world. One commented, for example, that "the academy continues to be at the center of wide-ranging sociopolitical issues that are shaping the world" (Respondent 36). Among these issues, as noted by the respondents, were "push[ing] back on systemic injustices" (Respondent 4) and ensuring "a lively and effective democracy" (Respondent 37). Engagement of student affairs organizations, and the leaders themselves, in making a difference in addressing these critical matters for individuals as well as the communities in which they live and the larger society was a source of excitement for our respondents.

### Increasing Diversity

> [I'm excited by] students accessing higher education, in ever-greater numbers, from a rich array of cultural groups and life experiences. They bring resilience, humility, hunger for learning, and respect for wisdom. Students in colleges and universities today give me hope for the future of humanity. (Respondent 15)

Our respondents valued the opportunities to make a difference presented by the increasing diversity of students in higher education. First-generation students, low-income students, and other students mentioned by the leaders as historically marginalized in higher education (e.g., transgender students, students with disabilities) were named specifically as the foci of exciting changes in contemporary colleges and universities.

Opportunities to make a difference included changing cultures of inequity and exclusion, both on campus and off, including to "require/compel college and university campuses to consider strengthening cultural competencies" (Respondent 31). Students first need to feel welcome on campus and have the support networks and safety nets to allow them to find a sense of belonging and comfort-ability. Our respondents noted the importance of accurately assessing students' most basic needs of safety and security while looking ahead to their successful completion of course of study and making a successful transition from the institution. The leaders' comments are consistent with recent higher education scholarship on creating multicultural and inclusive communities on contemporary campuses (see Watt, 2015; Watt & Linley, 2014; Winkle-Wagner & Locks, 2014) and provide hopeful insights into the priorities of these student affairs leaders.

### The Promise of Technology and Social Media

> Social media gives (sic) us a tool with which to connect around the world ... and increase awareness about what students need. I am excited about this tool as a way to provide thought leadership, to amplify the voices of students and professionals, and to mobilize all of us to places of strength in our individual and collective work. (Respondent 1)

The challenges of expanding digital technologies and social media that we discussed in the previous chapter were, for some of our respondents, counterbalanced by the promise those technologies hold for increasing students' learning, institutional effectiveness, and social change (see Carey, 2015; Smith, Rainie, & Zickuhr, 2011). Responsible use of the technologies—by students, campuses, and media outlets—was seen as a way to improve access to higher education for students who might be ill-served by traditional models of education, to communicate more effectively with students about matters of importance to students and institutions; and to communicate more effectively with communities and stakeholders off campus. At the same time, it is important to note that some students might, due to their economic circumstances and/or family background, need assistance in catching up with students who had access to digital and educational technologies from a very young age.

**Summary.** The student affairs leaders' responses were replete with examples of their desire and commitment to make a difference, not only in the lives of students, but also in the educational quality and overall effectiveness of their institutions and to the benefit of broader national and global priorities. They embraced the challenges of creating inclusive multicultural communities, promoting ideals of social justice, and using digital technologies and social media to improve student learning and access to success. To be effective in creating environments and to yield productive outcomes, student affairs leaders are going to need to cross traditional boundaries to garner assistance and expertise from those involved directly with community service, civic engagement, social media, and IT.

### Collaboration and Community

> I ... am excited about the opportunities student affairs has to engage in the academic mission of the university and work with faculty colleagues to make their classrooms the place for engagement ... We can help them create community in their classroom ... (Respondent 5)

When describing what kept them going, student affairs leaders offered many examples of collaboration and community, including partnerships on campus and teamwork and collegiality within student affairs organizations as well as academic affairs, alumni, and development, and community partnerships (including nonprofit agencies and town and city offices).

### Campus Partnerships

> The opportunities to connect academic learning and co-curricular experience are broader than ever before (in my experience). ... We are having energizing conversations with faculty, with employers, and with academic administrators, and there is a sense of positive momentum here. (Respondent 52)

Our respondents expressed excitement about opportunities to work across organizational divisions and schools within their institutions, particularly with academic partners. The student affairs leaders described academic and student affairs partnerships founded on shared commitment to student success and aimed at developing seamless living and learning environments for students.

A strength of these collaborations was their capacity to increase creativity, knowledge, expertise, and effectiveness. One respondent wrote, for example, about "breakthroughs when people find ways to connect with others who are ready to work in new ways" (Respondent 38). Another noted "a greater appreciation on my campus for what student affairs does, what contributions we make, and for what future we can co-create for our institution" (Respondent 9).

Campus partnerships, especially those joining academic and student affairs together in efforts to improve student learning, have received considerable attention in higher education and student affairs literature (Whitt, 2010). Examples extolling the benefits of such partnerships (see Cook & Lewis, 2007), noting their complexities (see Arcelus, 2011; Magolda, 2005), and demonstrating their impact (see Kezar & Lester, 2009; Whitt, Elkins Nesheim, Guentzel, Kellogg, McDonald, & Wells, 2008) are plentiful. The "on-the-ground" experiences of our respondents offer some evidence to reinforce the usefulness of these collaborations, and they also reinforce the satisfying impact they can have on their participants.

### Collaborations Within Student Affairs

> I have a dynamic structure that includes all of student affairs, enrollment management, athletics, advancement, alumni relations and marketing/communications. This model affords us the opportunity to look at prospects/students/alums and others through a life cycle of engagement. As a result, collaboration, communication, teamwork, and productivity are enhanced. It's great! (Respondent 12)

Our respondents also enjoyed partnerships with their colleagues in student affairs. They praised their "smart, capable, talented" (Respondent 33) staff members and expressed gratitude for the opportunity to hire and develop the skills of these "deeply committed" (Respondent 46) people. Student affairs leaders also described the excitement of leading a team of caring and energetic people working together to fulfill a common vision and commitment for student learning and student success. Teamwork aimed at changing organizational culture and empowering community members also provided satisfaction for our respondents.

**New Professionals**

> The next generation of practitioners gives me much hope and excites me. They are much better prepared for this work than we were at the same points in our careers. That's a testament to our generation, though, who have made the commitment to provide our younger colleagues with a breadth and depth of professional development not available to most of us now in the senior positions. They recognize the challenges we will bequeath to them and are actually energized to find solutions to them. Bless their hearts! (Respondent 39)

Comments from several of our respondents drew attention to one group of staff members in particular: new student affairs professionals. The student affairs leaders were excited about the idealism, enthusiasm, and commitment to change they see in their junior colleagues. One noted "The commitment of young professionals to continuing to broaden access to college is admirable" (Respondent 28).

In the book *Job One 2.0* (Magolda & Carnaghi, 2014), new professionals tell their own stories about their transitions from graduate school to their first professional positions. Their stories highlight and emphasize themes of relationships, fit, competence, and confidence. Some of the new professionals' themes are timeless, yet their lives have also become increasingly more complicated as well as potentially more interesting with contemporary issues layered upon what our respondents experienced as young professionals. Magolda and Carnaghi (2014) noted some of the changes new professionals are facing.

> *Job One 2.0* stories implicitly and explicitly discuss the impact of the economy, the influence of outside forces on student affairs, technology, and shifting demographics on their job searches and job duties, revealing unique, inescapable, contemporary, and contested issues—topics worth of consideration, dialogue, and action. (page xvii)

As our respondents noted, they are most interested and excited about who is going to come after them and the impact these new professionals will have on the profession, their institutions, and the lives of students. So, of course, they have a commitment to ensuring the next generation of student affairs professionals' success—just as they have expressed a similar commitment to their work with students. Both students and new professionals require our respondents to stay current and up-to-date on these two constituents' wants and needs and most likely affect how our respondents go about prioritizing their time.

### Community Engagement

> I am excited about the broadening of our campus borders to include the community and the powerful learning that can take place through community and civic engagement. (Respondent 9)

Some of our respondents included expanding the borders of campus, both through institutional outreach and student engagement, in what excited them about collaborations and partnerships. This is consistent with the student affairs leaders' commitment to the power of education to transform lives and communities.

**Summary.** The concepts of community, community development, collaboration have been around for a long, long time. Our respondents took these concepts, or themes, to the next level and realized and expressed that true, ongoing partnerships need to be started, nurtured, and promoted to ensure not only student learning and student success but also to promote organizational stability and to explore ways to work smarter and more in unison (or centralized) with multiple parts of the institution. The time for hunkering down, insulating oneself or one's division, and creating one's own fiefdom is past. With shrinking financial resources and greater scrutiny of the cost of higher education, colleges and universities can no longer afford (figuratively and literally) to solve their problems by the additive model—adding more staff, creating another specialized unit, or subdividing units. Student affairs organizations need to work to connect with faculty and to become boundary spanners—bringing disparate parts together to create forums for brainstorming, discussion, and problem solving.

### Leading and Facilitating Change

> [What keeps me going is] change—new projects, which are exciting, new building projects, other new initiatives which will benefit our students. (Respondent 49)

> Innovation ... keeps me going as it demonstrates that there are unique approaches to the challenges of the day ... It requires us to pull on a variety of skills and knowledge and to also examine the issue in a different way. I guess it feeds my inner geek. (Respondent 44)

Earlier in this chapter, we described the enthusiasm of our respondents for making a difference for students and their communities through the transformative power of education. The student affairs leaders also found excitement in opportunities to make a difference in the organizations in which they work and lead. Some of their comments addressed changes in student affairs organizations and some focused on change at the institutional level.

### Institutional Change

> [I'm excited by] organizational changes and challenges. [I take] a general manager's approach to building the right team of "subject matter experts," weaving these talents to greater heights to promote the university's mission and aspirations. [I can help] solve problems at all levels of the institution, especially with cabinet colleagues that cross all segments of university life and viability. (Respondent 18)

The student affairs leaders found satisfaction in being able to have an impact within their organizations and on their institutions and described excitement about the possibilities for change through new programs and practices, and more importantly, for innovative solutions to challenging problems. Several also mentioned opportunities for capital improvements, including new residence halls. Our respondents grounded change efforts in an overarching commitment to being a part of achieving their institutional missions, including student success.

### Change in Student Affairs

> ...I am...excited, albeit nervous, about the prospects of rethinking student affairs organizations and practice to align better with the critical objectives and outcomes that our institutions have for student learning, development, and overall success. (Respondent 9)

The student affairs leaders also found satisfaction in effecting change in how student affairs is organized and functions on their campuses. Their statements demonstrated enthusiasm for creating inclusive and dynamic structures—again, in collaboration with campus partners—that bridge stereotypical silos of academic and student affairs.

As noted under Collaboration and Community, calls for more integrated college and university structures increase as evidence mounts regarding the importance of seamless living and learning environments for student success and as institutional resources shrink (Blumenstyk, 2015; Kuh et al., 2005, 2010). Student affairs organizations also have been called upon to operate more effectively to facilitate student learning and development (see Kuh et al., 2005, 2010). Increasing specialization of student affairs' functions can work against both productive collaborations within and outside of student affairs organizations and efforts to create holistic student experiences within student affairs (Porterfield, Roper, & Whitt, 2011; Task Force on the Future of Student Affairs, 2010). This is a concern noted by our respondents as well. See, for example, the statement by Respondent 20 in Chapter 2 (see page 32). It also was noted as a reason for excitement by one of our respondents, who talked about "putting to rest traditional student affairs that has historically bifurcated curricular and co-curricular life in favor of a far more integrated model" (Respondent 45).

**Summary.** Change—leading and facilitating change, seeing changes occur in institutions and student affairs units—was a consistent theme in our respondents' statements about what kept them going. Their comments communicated a sense of energy and dynamism about finding innovative and creative solutions to structural, financial, and educational challenges their organizations face.

## Learning, Data, and Scholarship

> If (some would say when) there is a large-scale move to performance-based funding, we are really going to have to show how we contribute to retention, graduation, and time to degree—not just have a philosophical "belief" that we do based on our anecdotal experiences. These are real opportunities to change the way we think, the way we do our work, the ways we influence and create policy. (Respondent 5)

Consistent with their excitement about leading change and making a difference were the student affairs leaders' comments about being learners themselves, and using data and evidence to make decisions.

### Leaders as Learners

> Reading about current issues in the field is also energizing. It helps me remember to always be a student of this discipline. That role is as critical as my role as a leader. This is my belief because, in my estimation, lack of evolution by learning = lack of effective leadership. (Respondent 22)

> [What keeps me going is I] learn something every day, not to mention I am having fun. (Respondent 50)

Learning was something that kept our respondents going, not just student learning, but learning as part of the role of a leader in an educational institution. Staying current with research, scholarship, and current events in higher education and student affairs was noted as both exciting and essential. Some also commented on the importance of engaging in scholarly activities themselves, and were excited by opportunities their roles offered for that engagement.

### Data for Effectiveness

[I'm excited by] possibilities of harnessing analytics (learning, predictive, etc.) to inform student success practice. We have SO MUCH data on SO MANY things that it's unethical NOT to use it in service of student success. (Respondent 38)

[I'm excited about] all the successes we have had and the potential for more. As a community college SSAO, I'm looking at metrics such as retention and graduation rates and student grades. By using student learning and development theory to guide our work, we have already moved the needle in the right direction. (Respondent 41)

Our respondents voiced strong support for increasing demands for outcomes assessment, program evaluation, and the use of data to inform decisions about allocating resources. They were excited that, as one stated, "outcomes and assessment are holding us more accountable to the work we should be doing" (Respondent 31). Another noted, "we know more than ever!" (Respondent 2) about students' needs, expectations, behavior, and experiences, providing more opportunities than ever to create responsive programs and practices. Accreditation standards calling for clear learning outcomes and assessment of those outcomes also were seen as a way to demonstrate student affairs' achievements and to bring student affairs organizations into closer alignment with institutional priorities and the academic mission.

**Summary.** The student affairs leaders also were learners. They learned from research and writing about higher education and student affairs, and they learned from institutional data. In addition, our respondents described myriad ways they used what they learned so they and their organizations could be more effective.

## Our Work

I leap from my bed every morning grateful to do this work—our work matters, has meaning, is both empathic and strategic. (Respondent 13)

[What keeps me going] is being challenged every day, willing to take risks, have fun, and enjoy what life brings. (Respondent 12)

Woven through the student affairs leaders' statements about what keeps them going was a thread of joy—joy in the work of student affairs; the work of leading institutions and student affairs organizations to greater effectiveness; the work of making a difference for students, their campuses, and the world. But, as we have noted elsewhere, their excitement seemed to be more about the whole than the sum of those parts, more about the work than as a set of roles and responsibilities. This was not surprising—after all, we did ask them what they found exciting—but the frequency with which they used words such as "love," "joy," "inspiration," and "fun" was fun to read.

They loved the diversity of their jobs, which allowed them to use many skills and a wide range of expertise, and provided them with tremendous variety in how they spent their time. As one noted, opportunities "to lead groups, to complete detail-oriented reports, to connect with students, to work with and supervise a fantastic staff team, and to use creativity to address needs—It's also fun!" (Respondent 10).

The work the leaders loved also explicitly included the challenges that troubled them because those challenges required them to make a difference and to draw on the ideals and values that always have sustained them, "the purposefulness of the core work" (Respondent 21). For example, one of the respondents was excited at being "in the middle of the conflict [rather] than standing on the sidelines" (Respondent 50).

**Summary.** Our respondents took joy, inspiration, and energy from their work. That work encompasses students and their learning and development, opportunities to make a difference to people and organizations, and the variety comprising student affairs leadership. Comments about "the work" also reflected, and were embedded in, the values, purposes, and aspirations that drew the student affairs leaders to student affairs work in the first place. In Chapter 4, we return to the topic of the "core work"—the values and ideals of student affairs—as we examine the implications of what we learned from our respondents' troubling and exciting experiences.

## Conclusion

At the end of Chapter 2, as they reflected on what our respondents said troubled them, Larry Roper and Elizabeth Whitt referred to the roles of student affairs leaders as "increasingly weighty and complex," confronted with "powerful social forces," "insufficient resources," and "inadequate institutional support." As we conclude this chapter, we do not take issue with that characterization of the challenges the leaders face. It is, however, incomplete.

The student affairs leaders' statements about what excited them and kept them going provide the rest of the story. Their weighty and complex roles are grounded in a deep love for the work those roles embody. They confront their difficult challenges with an abiding commitment to making a difference for the students who are at the center of their work. And they find joy and inspiration in those students and their learning and development. We explore these issues further in Chapter 4 as we discuss what the experiences of the student affairs leaders can mean for understanding and shaping student affairs leadership. Before moving on to that discussion, however, we conclude with the words of yet another respondent:

> It's still the best job in the world. To be surrounded by bright young minds each and every day—to be challenged and affirmed by what they're doing. (Respondent 29)

## References

Arcelus, V. J. (2011). If student affairs–academic affairs collaboration is such a good idea, why are there so few examples of these partnerships in American higher education? In P. M. Magolda & M. B. Baxter Magolda (Eds.), *Contested issues in student affairs: Diverse perspectives and respectful dialogue* (pp. 61–74). Sterling, VA: Stylus.

Arum, R., & Roksa, J. (2011). *Academically adrift: Limited learning on college campuses.* Chicago, IL: University of Chicago Press.

Blumenstyk, G. (2015). *American higher education in crisis? What everyone needs to know.* New York, NY: Oxford University Press.

Carey, K. (2015). *The end of college: Creating the future of learning and the university of everywhere.* New York, NY: Riverhead.

Cook, J. H., & Lewis, C. A. (Eds.). (2007). *Student and academic affairs collaboration: The divine comity.* Washington, DC: National Association of Student Personnel Administrators.

Keeling, R. P., & Hersh, R. H. (2011). *We're losing our minds: Rethinking American higher education.* New York, NY: Palgrave Macmillan.

Kezar, A., & Lester, J. (2009). *Organizing higher education for collaboration: A guide for campus leaders.* San Francisco, CA: Jossey-Bass.

Kuh, G. D., & Ikenberry, S. (2009). *More than you think, less than we need: Learning outcomes assessment in American higher education.* Champaign, IL: National Institute for Learning Outcomes Assessment.

Kuh, G. D., Kinzie, J. I., Schuh, J. H., Whitt, E. J. & Associates. (2005, 2010). *Student success in college: Creating conditions that matter.* San Francisco, CA: Jossey-Bass.

Lumina Foundation for Education. (2009). *Goal 2025: Lumina Foundation's strategic plan.* Indianapolis, IN: Author.

Magolda, P. M. (2005). Proceed with caution: Uncommon wisdom about academic and student affairs partnerships. *About Campus, 9*(6), 16–21.

Magolda, P.M., & Carnaghi, J.E. (2014). *Job one 2.0: Understanding the next generation of student affairs professionals.* 2d ed. Lanham, MD: University Press of America.

Porterfield, K. T., Roper, L. D., & Whitt, E. J. (2011). Redefining our mission: What does higher education need from student affairs? *Journal of College & Character, 12*(4), 1–7.

Smith, A., Rainie, L., & Zickuhr, K. (2011, July 11). College students and technology. Pew Research Center. Retrieved from http://www.pewinternet.org/2011/07/19/college-students-and-technology/

Task Force on the Future of Student Affairs. (2010). *Envisioning the future of student affairs: Final report of the task force on the future of student affairs.* Washington, DC: ACPA & NASPA.

Watt, S. K. (Ed.). (2015). *Designing transformative multicultural initiatives: Theoretical foundations, practical applications, and facilitator considerations.* Sterling, VA: Stylus.

Watt, S. K., & Linley, J. (Eds.). (2014). Creating successful multicultural initiatives in higher education and student affairs. *New Directions for Student Services, No. 144.* San Francisco, CA: Jossey-Bass.

Whitt, E. J. (2010). Academic and student affairs partnerships. In J. H. Schuh, S. R. Jones, & S. R. Harper (Eds.) *Student services: A handbook for the profession* (5th ed.). San Francisco, CA: Jossey-Bass.

Whitt, E. J., Elkins Nesheim, B. S., Guentzel, M. J., Kellogg, A. H., McDonald, W. M., & Wells, C. A. (2008). "Principles of good practice" for academic and student affairs partnership programs. *Journal of College Student Development, 49*(3), 235–249.

Winkle-Wagner, R., & Locks, A. M. (2014). *Diversity and inclusion on campus: Supporting racially and ethnically underrepresented students.* New York, NY: Routledge.

ELIZABETH J. WHITT *is vice provost and dean for undergraduate education and professor in sociology at University of California, Merced.*

JILL E. CARNAGHI *is assistant vice president for student development at Saint Louis University.*

4

*This chapter describes and discusses implications of the experiences of student affairs leaders—the challenges and the opportunities, the obstacles and the joy—for understanding and facilitating student affairs leadership.*

# Embracing Core Values: Finding Joy in the Challenges of our Work

*Larry D. Roper, Kent T. Porterfield, Elizabeth J. Whitt, Jill E. Carnaghi*

> I enjoy this work, [a] calling if you will, as much as ever, as it is a privilege to have a role that draws on so many aspects, interests, and abilities while never failing to expose my inadequacies. (Respondent 18)

In Chapters 2 and 3, we described the data provided by the student affairs leaders, both what troubled them and what excited them. In this chapter, we focus on possible ramifications of those data. We begin by examining some themes across the data, noting and discussing tensions and seeming inconsistencies. We return then to the core values of student affairs work described in Chapter 1 as a way to make meaning of the challenges and opportunities in our respondents' experiences and to identify implications for contemporary student affairs leadership.

## Considering Janus and Other Complications

In the quotation above, Respondent 18 humorously conveys a contradiction in the role of a student affairs leader: exciting opportunities that draw consistently on extensive capacities while consistently revealing limitations. Looking across the data from all our respondents, we see many examples of similar contradictions.

According to the ancient Romans, Janus—for whom January was named—was the god of transitions and beginnings; he typically was portrayed as having two heads looking in opposite directions, one to the future and the other to the past (Kuh & Whitt, 1987). In organizational studies, Janusian thinking described the ability of persons within organizations to maintain contradictory thoughts simultaneously, an ability that created openness to possibilities and complicated ways of thinking about problems and solutions (Kuh & Whitt, 1987; Weick, 1979). The notion of Janusian thinking was helpful to us as we examined the contradictions that might be discerned in the experiences presented by our respondents.

The student affairs leaders painted a vivid picture of their experiences that revealed complex, intense, and ambiguous roles influenced strongly by rapidly evolving circumstances within and outside their institutions; internal and external political agendas; changing student characteristics and needs; complicated relationships with colleagues and campus partners; and competing commitments. The spectrum of issues for which the student affairs leaders were responsible ranged from deep engagement with individual students, to management of administrative processes associated with externally imposed mandates, to leadership for strategic institutional priorities. They participated in activities that involved planning for change and activities that placed them in reactive positions. Our respondents described their roles in ways that suggested there are dynamic tensions constantly at play: thought versus action, planning versus reacting, avoidance versus engagement, collaboration versus isolation, and control versus chaos. Their work was a mix of task and process, crisis and routine, teaching others and personal learning, community and individual engagement, and many other seemingly dichotomous streams. They were pulled and pushed, encouraged and frustrated, stressed and energized, filled with angst and filled with joy. Perhaps what seems paradoxical might, in fact, be the nature of student affairs leadership: opportunities are challenges and challenges are opportunities.

As we mentioned in the previous chapters, there were a number of specific experiences and issues described by the student affairs leaders as both keeping them up at night—that is, troubling them—and keeping them going—that is, exciting them. We discuss two here, as illustrations. First, social media and digital technologies were viewed as creating barriers to community and communication. At the same time, our respondents felt social media and digital technologies created opportunities for effective communication to and from students and for forming new and productive communities of learners, both on campus and off.

Second, increasing student diversity, and the calls for creating inclusive communities to support and benefit from that diversity, also were seen as both troubling and exciting. To be clear, the student affairs leaders were *not* troubled by diversity and inclusion. They were, however, kept up at night by the tremendous challenges they and their institutions faced in supporting and honoring the contributions of students previously underrepresented in higher education, as well as the challenges of fostering inclusive multicultural communities. Nevertheless, those challenges created opportunities for making a difference in the lives of students, institutions, the nation, and the world—a consistent source of excitement and energy for the respondents.

Despite these tensions, our respondents were inspired by the hopefulness that came from the power and potential of education to transform students' lives; the wonders of community; the promise of leadership; and affection for a vocation that is grounded in core values of care, inclusion, social justice, and service. Although these varied and uneven undercurrents and the daily work activities associated with them can appear disjointed, the student affairs leaders faced bringing coherence to the mix of issues and expectations assigned to them and for which they were held accountable.

What should we make of those, and other, possible contradictions in the respondents' experiences? We could, perhaps, find ways to make the seeming inconsistencies seem consistent. The aforementioned Janusian thinking encouraged us to keep looking in both directions and resist attempts at a single view (Kuh & Whitt, 1987; Weick, 1979). Consistent with that approach, we looked back and found old, but timely, advice from several organizational scholars. More than 40 years ago, in their book about the ambiguities of presidential leadership in colleges and universities, Michael Cohen and James March wrote, "Interesting people and interesting organizations construct complicated theories of themselves" (Cohen & March, 1974, p. 223). From the perspective of complicated theories of interesting people and organizations, efforts to reduce ambiguity and resolve contradictions are futile, even undesirable. Several years later, organizational psychologist Karl Weick echoed Cohen and March when he urged leaders and students of organizations to "Complicate yourself!" (Weick, 1979, p. 259). We believed that was good advice decades ago, and now it seemed appropriate for making meaning of current student affairs leaders' experiences and student affairs leadership. We continue to look backward and forward to "complicate ourselves" throughout the rest of this chapter.

## Revisiting Core Values and Contemporary Challenges

In Chapter 1, Kent Porterfield and Elizabeth Whitt provided a brief overview of documents, for example, the *Student Personnel Point of View* (American Council on Education [ACE], 1937), *Tomorrow's Higher Education [T.H.E.] Project* (American College Personnel Association [ACPA], 1975), Brown (1972), *Student Learning Imperative* (ACPA, 1994), *Principles of Good Practice for Student Affairs* (ACPA & National Association of Student Personnel Administrators [NASPA], 1997), and *Envisioning the Future of Student Affairs* (Task Force on the Future of Student Affairs [Task Force], 2010) that were developed at critical points in the history of American higher education for the purpose of examining the role of student affairs at those points and beyond. Taken together, the documents that traced the development of student affairs work iterated, and reiterated, the core values of the field in remarkably consistent terms. The *Principles of*

*Good Practice for Student Affairs* (ACPA & NASPA, 1997) document, produced by a study group appointed by ACPA and NASPA, provides a useful summary:

> Values evident across the history of student affairs work include an acceptance and appreciation of individual differences; lifelong learning; education for effective citizenship; student responsibility; ongoing assessment of learning and performance (students' and our own); pluralism and multiculturalism; ethical and reflective student affairs practice; supporting and meeting the needs of students as individuals and in groups; and freedom of expression with civility. (ACPA & NASPA, 1997, p. 2)

Dedication to these core values was clear throughout the comments of our respondents. They were explicit about the energy and good feelings they derived from the aspects of their roles that allowed them to engage with student growth, exercise leadership, and facilitate change. They also described their commitment to building strong, diverse, and just communities, and to achieving the educational missions of their institutions. The enduring values of the student affairs profession remained a major source of what excited and inspired the student affairs leaders.

Moreover, the student affairs leaders' comments also reflected the great challenges of current American higher education, just as those defining student affairs documents reflected their historical contexts. We believe, however, that none of those documents captures the intensity and complexity of the issues faced by today's student affairs leaders, nor how our respondents experienced those issues. The student affairs leaders expressed that they are dealing with more complicated issues under more intense scrutiny and with higher expectations for accountability than at any other time. The current landscape surely has deepened the intensity of student affairs leadership, while also broadening the number of stakeholders who are invested in what student affairs work is and how it is performed.

There is nothing to indicate the pace and consequences of change will subside. As they do today, student affairs leaders will continue to face externally—and internally—motivated mandates, shrinking resources, and calls for accountability. However, these situations are likely to become more complex and demands to address them more urgent, even as the conditions for leadership become more tumultuous and less certain. The enormity of the challenges student affairs leaders will face in forging and sustaining clear pathways to student and institutional success amid the clamor of competing priorities and uncertainties of constant change cannot be overstated.

Thus, student affairs leaders must find ways to lead within the turbulent contexts of their work. Successful leadership for the future requires that student affairs leaders bring harmony to those aspects of their work that feel paradoxical or puzzling, while allowing themselves to "construct complicated theories of themselves" (Cohen & March, 1974, p. 223) and resist urges to seek simple solutions to complex problems.

**Rethinking student affairs, redux.** For assistance identifying ways to address those leadership challenges, we turn again to student affairs history, both the calls to action and the core values. We believe they still are relevant to student affairs leadership in what management expert Peter Vaill described many years ago as "permanent white water ... you never get out of the rapids" (Vaill, 1989, p. 2). For example, according to the *Student Learning Imperative* (ACPA, 1994),

> Student affairs must model what we wish for our students: an ever increasing capacity for learning and self-reflection. By redesigning its work with these aims in mind, student affairs will significantly contribute to realizing the institution's mission and students' educational and personal aspirations. (ACPA, p. 5)

In a similar vein, the authors of the *Principles of Good Practice* (ACPA & NASPA, 1997) asserted,

> Today's context for higher education presents student affairs with many challenges ... Our response to these challenges will shape our role in higher education. The choice of student affairs educators is simple: We can pursue a course that engages us in the central mission of our institutions or retreat to the margins in the hope that we will avoid the inconvenience of change. (ACPA & NASPA, p. 1)

And the authors of *Envisioning the Future of Student Affairs* (Task Force, 2010) stated,

> Although the history of the field is replete with calls for forward-thinking and risk-taking in the name of doing student affairs work in new ways under new conditions ... [in] many instances we greet change by doing what we have always done, only better. At no time in history has the incentive for real change been more powerful or the consequences of not changing more significant. The field's ability to survive and thrive rests on our willingness to look at our work in a new light ... (Task Force, 2010, p. 7)

All of these documents asserted, strongly, that familiar, comfortable practices of the past are inadequate for conditions of unprecedented change and uncertainty. All raised calls to action for student affairs leaders, both on campuses and in professional associations, with a similar message: Think and act in fundamentally different ways about student affairs work (e.g., programs, practices, roles, structures, assumptions, and cultures) so as to engage effectively at the heart of student and institutional success.

Those documents also point, however, to the core values of the student affairs field for grounding and shaping the process and content of rethinking of student affairs work. Again, we offer an example from *Envisioning the Future of Student Affairs* (Task Force, 2010), which urged student affairs leaders to "never lose sight of the fundamental purpose for which your work exists and the core values that it honors" (Task Force, p. 13).

Before we say more about these calls to action and our thoughts about their implications, as well as implications of our respondents' experiences, for contemporary and future student affairs leadership, we need to stop to provide a few words in the interest of full disclosure. Two authors of this sourcebook, Larry Roper and Elizabeth Whitt, were members of the study group that developed *Principles of Good Practice for Student Affairs* (ACPA & NASPA, 1997). Three authors of this sourcebook, Kent Porterfield, Larry Roper, and Elizabeth Whitt, were members of the Task Force on the Future of Student Affairs, the group that prepared *Envisioning the Future of Student Affairs* (Task Force, 2010). Now we find ourselves revisiting, and reiterating, our past statements – some almost 20 years past—about the need for rethinking student affairs work in times of great change and challenge. Therefore, we have to wonder whether we are the embodiment of the saying that insanity is doing the same thing over and over again, expecting a different result, or an example of the persistence Cohen and March (1974) endorsed for leadership under conditions of ambiguity: "The loser who persists in a variety of contexts is frequently rewarded" (p. 208). In any case, we believe there is scant evidence that those calls to action—calls to rethink student affairs work—have been effective, yet we continue.

We recognize there are many ways to "rethink" student affairs leadership. The documents described above and others (see Blimling, Whitt et al., 1999; Kuh et al., 2005, 2010; Kuh, Kinzie, Schuh, & Whitt, 2011; Manning, Kinzie, & Schuh, 2014; Porterfield, Roper, & Whitt, 2011; Whitt, 1999) call for thinking differently about, and making significant changes in assumptions, purposes, roles, organizational structures, and so on. Those resources also provide specific suggestions for how student affairs work and leadership can be rethought; we refer you to any or all of them for further study as we will not spend more time on that topic here.

However, although we have not given up on the desirability, even necessity, of significant changes in how student affairs work is organized and performed, we offer two other approaches for rethinking student affairs leadership in times of change: (a) reframing perspectives of leaders, and (b) reaffirming the core values of student affairs.

## Reframing the Work

Early in this chapter, we examined potential contradictions in our respondents' descriptions of what they found troubling and exciting and resolved to "complicate ourselves" (see Weick, 1979). In this section, we further complicate ourselves, and student affairs leadership, by considering ways student affairs leaders might make different meanings of their experiences by reframing those experiences. We argue that complicating oneself requires bringing new interpretations to what one assumes is reality. We further argue that "believing is seeing ... [that] interpretation of experience depends not only on what we see, but also on what we expect to see and what the common frame of reference or world view encourages us to see" (Kuh & Whitt, 1987, pp. ix and x).

A frame "is a mental model—a set of assumptions that you carry in your head to help you understand and negotiate a particular 'territory'" (Bolman & Deal, 2013, p. 10). Thus, frames are perceptual maps, largely tacit ways of understanding and making meaning of one's world (Bolman & Deal, 2013). A classic example of the disadvantages of overusing one frame is in the saying, "To a three-year-old with a hammer, everything is a nail." (source unknown) Frames, or mental models, of student affairs leaders might include assumptions and expectations about how students learn, or what faculty members believe about how students learn, or how a student affairs organization must be structured, or how a student affairs leader should spend time, or even what leadership is (Arnold & Kuh, 1999).

To reframe, then, is to alter one's frames, thereby "thinking about situations in more than one way, which lets you develop alternative diagnoses and strategies" (Bolman & Deal, 2013, p. 5). Reframing is one way to develop deeper and more profound understandings of our experiences and of the systems and the circumstances in which we operate. One of the aims of reframing is to help leaders identify new ideas and approaches they can bring to their work. The Futures Task Force asked, for example, "What would student affairs 'look like' if it were organized for the success of today's students and today's higher education?" (Task Force, 2010, p. 8). Might such a student affairs organization have more generalists and fewer specialists, such as our Respondent 19 suggested?

On a less organizational, more individual level, another reframing task might involve re-examining beliefs, assumptions and expectations with regard to Title IX. One frame for making meaning of Title IX policies, one expressed by several of our respondents, is "Title IX comprises a set of legal mandates, responding to which interferes with my real work." What if that frame were replaced with "Title IX comprises a set of legal mandates that *is* my real work"? If Title IX mandates are viewed as the real work, not a barrier to the real work, then what? One possible outcome of that reframing effort is concentrating on nothing but Title IX mandates. Another, however, is creating room for learning, for making a difference, for fostering healthy communities, and for providing value-laden institutional leadership in every single action and interaction related to Title IX. This is not to say reframing is the act of putting on rose-colored glasses. Instead, in this case, reframing is the act of illuminating what matters most about one's work in the process of fulfilling one aspect of that work. What matters most also is the focus on our next approach to rethinking student affairs work.

Reframing could be one useful approach to rethinking student affairs work. Reframing asks, and allows, student affairs leaders to look at their challenges and opportunities through multiple frames that create new ways to make meaning of their experiences. By making different meaning, they might find different, even more productive, ways of understanding and implementing their responsibilities.

## Declaring and Affirming Core Values

Declaring and affirming core values might not seem to be another way to rethink student affairs leadership at all. However, when one faces constantly changing conditions and competing priorities as resources dwindle, it can be easy to lose sight of what matters most. In our respondents' comments about the issues that troubled them, we noted a searching for ways to realign what brought them joy with their approaches to what troubled them. We also noted some seeking ways to express a stronger voice and assert leadership at the institutional level and across the larger higher education landscape. We would argue that, as student affairs leaders attempt to chart new and productive futures for themselves, their organizations and the student affairs field, they must affirm and reinforce the core values that motivate their work. In addition, student affairs leaders—on campuses and in professional associations—must make sense of the current postsecondary landscape in ways that enable them to make clear and unequivocal declarations about those values. The task before student affairs leaders is not to simplify their work, but to bring wholeness to it in a way that reflects and honors its core values while responding to the contemporary concerns of higher education and society.

For example, in the days following the September 11, 2001 attacks on New York and Washington, DC, the American Medical Association (AMA) heard voices of its members requesting a reaffirmation of their shared responsibility to address the global human condition. In response to this call, the AMA drafted and adopted *The Declaration of Professional Responsibility* (AMA, 2001). According to the AMA, one of the purposes of the Declaration is to provide physicians with a common statement, "by which 21st century physicians can publicly uphold and celebrate the ideals that, throughout history, have inspired individuals to enter medicine" (http://www.ama-assn.org/ama/pub/physician-resources/medical-ethics/declaration-professional-responsibility.page?). The Declaration's "language reflects the historical moment in which it arises," because the time at which it was written "demanded a reaffirmation of professional ideals by the world community of physicians," and the document speaks to "physicians in their roles as clinicians, researchers, educators, and members of a civil society" (http://www.ama-assn.org/ama/pub/physician-resources/medical-ethics/declaration-professional-responsibility.page?).

Although we do not claim the issues facing higher education and the student affairs profession are comparable in gravity to the incidents of September 11, 2001, the AMA's response to those incidents can be instructive about what a profession can do to chart a course in response to seriously challenging times. So, as at other points of crisis and uncertainty in the history of student affairs, we think now might be a good time to articulate a set of declarations, statements of common values that can provide clarity for navigating the rapids of change and uncertainty. Therefore, we take the bold step of offering the following declarations about and for student affairs work and leadership, based on our respondents' experiences, as a jumping-off point for further discussion. Although we refer to these statements as declarations, they might be viewed more productively as debatable propositions or contestable assertions intended to provoke debate aimed at clarifying common commitments that can assist student affairs leaders to make meaning of the challenges they face and create pathways to address those challenges.

## Declarations (or Debatable Propositions) About Student Affairs Work and Student Affairs Leadership

1. Student affairs leaders will bring the core values of their work to frame, and reframe, the issues facing higher education and the profession. Although the complexity, intensity, and urgency of contemporary issues are unprecedented, each and every one of those issues can be viewed as consistent with and connected to the foundational values of the student affairs field and will be approached as such.
2. Student affairs leaders will claim a voice for students and their learning. Through leadership, scholarship, and professional development, student affairs leaders will assertively articulate the transformative role of higher education in the lives of students, their communities, and the world, and will demonstrate the centrality of student affairs work in achieving that transformation.
3. Student affairs leaders and their professional associations will actively influence the content and direction of legislative and regulatory mandates in ways that ensure individual student dignity and success and healthy communities. Increased public attention and scrutiny to important social and political issues on campuses will be viewed as opportunities to promote educational values and common commitments in ways that might not be possible without the spotlight of heightened public and political attention.
4. Student affairs leaders will provide leadership for timely and thoughtful response to *incidents* that disrupt their communities. At the same time, however, student affairs leaders will advocate

for timely and thoughtful institutional responses to the broader *issues*—the structural, organizational, and cultural elements of institutions—that create the climate for those incidents.
5. Student affairs leaders will re-examine their models of organization and practice and implement alternative models to serve more effectively the needs of increasingly diverse student groups, support the unique needs of every student, and serve more effectively the educational missions of their institutions.
6. Student affairs leaders will seize the opportunity presented by increasing student activism to support and advocate for students who take on power structures and cultures that have become deeply embedded and heavily invested in defending the status quo. Student affairs leaders will demonstrate the capacity to listen to students with love and from an ethic of care. Student affairs leaders will understand and communicate that students are claiming their voices and asserting their identities, and will respond with thoughtful and sincere leadership by providing real answers to real issues.
7. Student affairs leaders will learn from social media–supported activism and be more deliberate and intentional about creating and proliferating educational messages that speak profoundly to the critical learning outcomes and values that both define and undergird their institutions and their work.
8. Student affairs leaders will use, sustain, and expand the rich tradition of student affairs research, scholarship, evaluation, and assessment to improve teaching, learning, program design, and service delivery. Evidence from research, evaluation, and assessment will support decisions and allocation of resources.
9. Student affairs leaders will model an ethos of wellness that destigmatizes mental health issues and educates campus leaders about mind, body, and spirit issues that students must manage to realize higher education's promise and live productive lives.
10. Student affairs leaders will continue to elevate teaching and learning, student growth and development, and community building as the core elements of their work. In doing so, student affairs leaders will focus resources on programs, policies, and practices that foster student success and institutional excellence, defined by mission-centered objectives and outcomes. Student affairs leaders will reflect through their efforts that cultivating learning is the pathway to individual, community and social well-being.

These declarations are examples of possible responses to issues raised by our respondents, as well as our observations of the current state of student affairs work. We challenge leaders in student affairs to think about what declarations about the nature and values of their work would be productive for the student affairs field, as well as for leaders themselves, to respond to the contemporary and future challenges. This might be a productive challenge for the student affairs professional associations to come together to address, as they have done in the past. Student affairs leaders might want to bring the question close to home and ask themselves and what declarations they are prepared to make about their own leadership. They might also want to pose that question to their campus colleagues as a way to elicit discussions about common commitments. We think these and other such activities can provoke useful conversations about what matters most to student affairs leaders and about the alignment between the values they and their organizations profess and the values they live.

## Conclusion

We started our work on this sourcebook with an interest in examining trends, opportunities, and challenges for senior student affairs leaders. As we noted in Chapter 1, we began that examination with two questions. First, what are the challenges and opportunities facing contemporary student affairs leaders? Second, given what we know about the current state of higher education, how can we help to create a sustainable approach to student affairs leadership in a volatile environment that also maintains focus on creating and sustaining high-quality educational environments and experiences for students? The 53 student affairs leaders who responded so generously to our request for information provided articulate and provocative responses to our first question. To answer the second, we drew on their experiences and the rich history of student affairs work. At critical points of change and uncertainty in American higher education over the past 100 years, student affairs leaders have come together to focus on new ways to think about that work while affirming the values in which that work was, and is, rooted.

The current conditions for student affairs leaders are a powerful mix of the elements that our respondents cited as the attributes that drew them to the field: the joy of observing students growing and learning, rewards of engagement in life-giving relationship networks, satisfaction of making a difference in their communities and their world, and challenges in opportunities to build and promote organizational growth and effectiveness. On the other hand, many tasks have become embedded in the roles of student affairs leaders for which there is insufficient knowledge, time and/or resources to do the work as effectively as they would like. These new demands in the form of legislation, student characteristics, social dynamics, and technology are sources of challenge and worry, yet they also offer unprecedented opportunities to facilitate success for students and institutions.

Student affairs leaders have embarked on a journey that requires a graceful balance between the angst that comes with high-stakes and highly visible responsibilities and the joy and energy that come from grounding all of their roles in the field's enduring values. In this chapter, we offered several approaches to rethinking student affairs work that provides student affairs leaders some useful ways to achieve that balance as they face unprecedented challenges and opportunities. We hope that, in the process, we honored the experiences of our respondents.

## References

American College Personnel Association (ACPA). (1975). A student development model for student affairs in tomorrow's higher education. *Journal of College Student Personnel, 16,* 334–341.
American College Personnel Association (ACPA). (1994). *The student learning imperative: Implications for student affairs.* Washington, DC: Author.
American College Personnel Association (ACPA) and National Association of Student Personnel Administrators (NASPA). (1997). *Principles of good practice for student affairs.* Washington, DC: Authors.
American Council on Education (ACE). (1937). *The student personnel point of view: A report of a conference on the philosophy and development of student personnel work in colleges and universities* (American Council on Education Study, Series 1, Vol. 1, No. 3). Washington, DC: Author.
American Medical Association. (2001, December 4). *Declaration of professional responsibility.* Retrieved from http://www.cms.org/uploads/Declaration-of-Professional-Responsibility.pdf
Arnold, K., & Kuh, G. D. (1999). What matters in undergraduate education? Mental models, student learning, and student affairs. In E. J. Whitt (Ed.), *Student learning as student affairs work: Responding to our imperative* (pp. 11–34). Washington, DC: National Association of Student Personnel Administrators.
Blimling, G. S., Whitt, E. J., & Associates (1999). *Good practice in student affairs: Principles to foster learning.* San Francisco, CA: Jossey-Bass.
Bolman, L. G., & Deal, T. E. (2013). *Reframing organizations: Artistry, choice, and leadership.* 5th ed. San Francisco, CA: Jossey-Bass.
Brown, R.D. (1972). Student development in tomorrow's higher education: A return to the academy. (Student Personnel Series No. 16). Washington, DC: American College Personnel Association.
Cohen, M. D., & March, J. G. (1974). *Leadership and ambiguity: The American college president* (2nd ed.). Boston, MA: Harvard Business School Press.
Kuh, G. D., Kinzie, J., Schuh, J. H., & Whitt, E. J. (2011). Fostering student success in hard times. *Change, 43*(4), 13–19.
Kuh, G. D., Kinzie, J. I., Schuh, J. H., Whitt, E. J., & Associates. (2005, 2010). *Student success in college: Creating conditions that matter.* San Francisco, CA: Jossey-Bass.
Kuh, G. D., & Whitt, E. J. (1987). *Student affairs work, 2001: A paradigmatic odyssey.* ACPA Media No. 42. Alexandria, VA: American College Personnel Association.
Manning, K., Kinzie, J., & Schuh, J. H. (2014). *One size does not fit all: Traditional and innovative models of student affairs practice* (2nd ed.). New York, NY: Routledge.
Porterfield, K. T., Roper, L. D., & Whitt, E. (2011). Redefining our mission: What does higher education need from student affairs? *Journal of College & Character, 12*(4), 1–7.
Task Force on the Future of Student Affairs. (2010). *Envisioning the future of student affairs: Final report of the task force on the future of student affairs.* Washington, DC: ACPA & NASPA.

Vaill, P. B. (1989). *Managing as performing art: New ideas for a world of chaotic change.* San Francisco, CA: Jossey-Bass.
Weick, K. E. (1979). *The social psychology of organizing* (2nd ed.). Reading, MA: Addison-Wesley.
Whitt, E. J. (Ed.). (1999). *Student learning as student affairs work: Responding to our imperative.* Washington, DC: National Association of Student Personnel Administrator.

LARRY D. ROPER *is professor in the School of Language, Culture and Society at Oregon State University and coordinator, College Student Services Administration and Social Justice Minor.*

KENT T. PORTERFIELD *is vice president for student development at Saint Louis University.*

ELIZABETH J. WHITT *is vice provost and dean for undergraduate education and professor in sociology at University of California, Merced.*

JILL E. CARNAGHI *is assistant vice president for student development at Saint Louis University.*

# INDEX

ACE. *See* American Council on Education (ACE)
ACPA. *See* American College Personnel Association (ACPA)
Affordability, challenges related to, 20–21
American Association for Higher Education (AAHE), 10
American Association of Community Colleges, 10
American Association of State Colleges and Universities (ASCU), 10
American College Personnel Association (ACPA), 9, 10, 13, 14, 57–60
American Council on Education (ACE), 9, 10, 13, 57
American higher education, 9–10; challenges in, 9; characterizations of, in 2015, 12–13; critiques of, 11; current state of, 11–13; importance of, 12. *See also* Student affairs work
American Medical Association, 62
Andreas, R. E., 9
Appleton, J. R., 10
Arcelus, V. J., 45
Arnold, K., 61
Arum, R., 10, 41
Association of Public and Land-Grant Universities (APLU), 10
Atwell, R. H., 9

Barr, V., 23
Blimling, G. S., 13, 60
Blumenstyk, G., 10, 12, 34, 41, 48
Bolman, L. G., 61
Boyer Commission on Educating Undergraduates in the Research University, 10
Briggs, C. M., 10
Brown, R. D., 10, 13, 57
Business models of effectiveness, 34
Byrne, J. V., 10

Campus and student safety, concerns on, 23–24, 28
Campus conversations, 32–33

Campus partnerships, 45
Carey, K., 10, 44
Carnaghi, J. E., 8, 39, 46, 53, 55, 67
Changes, 47–48; in institutions, 48; in student affairs units, 48–49
Cheatham, H. E., 10
*The Chronicle of Higher Education* (Goldie Blumenstyk), 10
Cohen, M. D., 57, 58, 60
Collaborations within student affairs, 45–46
Community engagement, 47
Compliance with federal regulations, burdens of, 27–28
Complicated theories of interesting people and organizations, 57
Cook, J. H., 45
Core values of work, 57–58; declaring and affirming of, 62–63
Corporatization of college, 34
Cost of attendance, 20–21
*The Cost of Federal Regulatory Compliance at Colleges and Universities: A Multi-Institutional Study*, 27
Craig, R., 10

Data for effectiveness, use of, 50
Deal, T. E., 61
*The Declaration of Professional Responsibility*, 62
Digital technologies, 29, 56; impact of, 29–30; investment in, 30; promise of, 44; student use of, 30–31
Diversity and inclusion, challenges to, 25–26, 56

Education, transformative power of, 42–43
Elkins Nesheim, B. S., 45
*Envisioning the Future of Student Affairs* (report), 14, 57, 59, 60
External funding, 21

Financial costs of compliance, 27–28
First-generation students, 21, 29, 43

Food insecurity, 24
Frames, 61

Gray, P., 23
Griggs, B., 26
Guentzel, M. J., 45
Gun violence on campuses, 23–24

Hartocollis, A., 26
Henriques, G., 23
Hersh, R. H., 10
Higher education: increasing diversity of students in, 43; power of, 42–43. *See also* American higher education
Historically underrepresented students, access for, 21–22, 43
Homelessness, 24

Ikenberry, S., 41
Inclusion needs of students, 25–26
Instagram, 30
Institutions' response to diversity, 26

Janusian thinking, 55–57
*Job One 2.0,* 46
Johnson, C. S., 10

Keeling, R. P., 10, 41
Kellogg, A. H., 45
Kezar, A., 45
Kinzie, J. I., 41, 48, 60
Krylowicz, B., 23
Kuh, G. D., 10, 41, 48, 55–57, 60, 61

Leaders, as learners, 49–50
Learning, student affairs leaders and, 49–50
Lester, J., 45
Lewis, C. A., 45
Linley, J., 43
Lloyd-Jones, E. M., 10
Locks, A. M., 43
Loughlin, S., 26, 31
Low-income students, 21, 43
Lumina Foundation for Education, 10, 41

Magolda, P. M., 45, 46
Manning, K., 60
March, J. G., 57, 58, 60
McDonald, W. M., 45

Mental health issues, 22–23
Mental models, 61
Mistler, B., 23
Mueller, K. H., 10

NASPA. *See* National Association of Student Personnel Administrators (NASPA)
National Association of State Universities and Land-Grant Colleges (NASULGC), 10
National Association of Student Personnel Administrators (NASPA), 9, 10, 13, 57–60
News agencies, 29

Obama, Barack, 12

Partnerships on campus, 45
Porterfield, K. T., 8, 9, 14, 17, 49, 55, 60, 67
*Principles of Good Practice for Student Affairs,* 13, 57–60
Professional identities, 34–35
Professional preparation, decline in, 35
Public trust, lack of, 28

Rainie, L., 30, 44
Reductionistic descriptions of students, 25
Reetz, D., 23
Reframing, 60–62
Resilience, decline in, 22–23
Rhatigan, J. J., 10
Roksa, J., 10
Roper, L. D., 8, 14, 19, 37, 49, 55, 60, 67

Saad, L., 24
Safety issues, 23–24, 28
Schuh, J. H., 9, 41, 48, 60
Sexual violence, 28
Shapiro, H., 12
Shedd, J. D., 10
Shirky, C., 10, 11
Smith, A., 30, 44
Social media, use and misuse of, 29–31, 64
Spending time with students, 40–41
Student affairs leaders, challenges faced by, 19–20, 58; access to success, 21–22; affordability and access, 20–22;

diversity and inclusion, 25–26; and leadership for future, 58; regulations and compliance, 27–29; student affairs leadership, 31–36; student health and well-being, 22–24; technology and media, 29–31. *See also* Study process

Student affairs leadership, concerns related to, 31–36; evidence of effectiveness, 33; organizational models, 33–34; professional performance and identity, 34–35; role and voice for student affairs, 32–33. *See also* Study process

Student affairs leaders, joys and inspirations for, 39–40; collaboration and community, 44–47; leading and facilitating change, 47–49; learning, data, and scholarship, 49–50; making a difference, 42–44; students, 40–42; work, 50–51. *See also* Study process

Student affairs organizations, 26, 41, 48–49

Student affairs professionals, new, 46

Student affairs work, 13–14, 50–51; ACPA-NASPA Task Force on rethinking on, 14–15; core values and contemporary challenges, 14, 57–58; declarations about, 63–65; and Janusian thinking, 55–57; reaffirming core values of student affairs, 62–63; redefining of, 15; reframing perspectives of leaders, 60–62; rethinking student affairs, 58–63. *See also* Study process

Student enrollment, decline in, 20

Student health and well-being, issues of, 22–24

*Student Learning Imperative,* 13, 57, 59

Student mental health, 22–23

*Student Personnel Point of View,* 13, 57

Students' college journeys, 41

Students of color, 21

Student success, 19, 41

Students with disabilities, 43

Study Group on the Conditions of Excellence in American Higher Education, 10

Study process, 1 (Appendix A), 5–6; data analysis, 2 (Appendix A); data collection, 1–2 (Appendix A); limitations, 4 (Appendix A); participants, 1 (Appendix A); respondents, 5–6 (Appendix B); responses on "What excites you?", 27–39 (Appendix D); responses on "What troubles you?", 7–26 (Appendix C); themes, 3–4 (Appendix A)

Task Force on Federal Regulation of Higher Education, 27

Task Force on the Future of Student Affairs, 10, 13, 14, 49, 57, 59–61

Teamwork, 45–46

Technology and media: challenges related to, 29–31; responsible use of, 44

Title IX, 28, 35, 61

*Tomorrow's Higher Education (T.H.E.) Project,* 13, 14, 57

Transformative power of education, 42–43

Transgender students, 43

Twitter, 29, 30

U.S. Department of Education, 10, 12

Vaill, P. B., 59

Violence, mental health and, 22–23

Voice for student affairs, 32–33, 63

Watt, S. K., 43

Weick, K. E., 56, 57, 60

Wells, C. A., 45

White House, 10

Whitt, E. J., 8–10, 13–15, 17, 19, 37, 39, 41, 45, 48, 49, 53, 55–57, 60, 61, 67

Winkle-Wagner, R., 43

Young student affairs professionals, 46

Zickuhr, K., 30, 44

# Appendix A

## Study Methods

As we noted more than a hundred pages ago, the idea for this sourcebook came from our experiences in student affairs and our interest in looking back and looking ahead at the nature of student affairs work. What follows is an overview of how we obtained the data discussed in this sourcebook. Participant selection and characteristics, data collection, and data analysis are described briefly. Note that we have not labeled this Appendix "Research Methods"; we do not claim to have used what any of us would consider to be rigorous research methods at any step of the project. We do, however, believe our participants provided useful information about their experiences, and we treated that information with rigor and respect in our analyses and interpretations.

## Participants

We contacted 70 senior student affairs officers in September 2015. In selecting the participants, we sought (a) a mix of public and private colleges and universities, (b) a mix of 2- and 4-year institutions (though the latter predominated), (c) geographic distribution within the United States, (d) breadth and depth of experience in student affairs and/or higher education professional and scholarly associations, and (e) range of experience in senior leadership roles, including at a single institution or at several. Some of the 70 were known to one or more of us, some were strangers to all of us, and three were coauthors of this sourcebook.

## Data Collection

Our request for assistance was sent via e-mail; the subject line for the message said *"New Directions for Student Services*: Seeking 8 Minutes of Your Time in the Next 8 Hours." We thought we might be more likely to get a response if we emphasized that we were not looking for lengthy or long-pondered information.

The message the respondents received from Elizabeth Whitt stated:

> Dear Colleague,
>
> I write on behalf of Jill Carnaghi, Kent Porterfield, Larry Roper and myself to request a (very) few minutes of your time today.
>
> We're preparing a *New Directions for Student Services* sourcebook on current leadership issues in student affairs, to be published in 2016. The book is intended to be a snapshot of the "state of the field of student affairs" at this

point in time from the perspective of leaders in the field. We're thinking of "Leading in a time of urgency" as a possible title ("Leading and surviving in permanent white water" was taken—with apologies to P. Vaill).

So, in keeping with that theme, what we seek from you are your quick responses—*immediate* reactions—to the following questions with regard to the current state of student affairs (e.g., in your work, in your institution, in the work you do in the preparation and development of staff, and so on—you decide):

What troubles you? What keeps you up at night?

What excites you? What keeps you going?

We know how busy you are and we thank you, in advance, for your help. We will share the results with you!

We received responses to our questions from 53 of the 70 people we contacted, a 75% response rate, which surprised and pleased us (the names and institutional affiliations of the respondents are provided in Appendix B). The 53 included 38 senior student affairs professionals, 12 faculty members (two emeritus), two full-time association professionals, and one university chancellor (who had extensive experience as a senior student affairs officer). They serve at community colleges (5), 4-year private universities (15), and 4-year public universities (31). Some have been in senior leadership roles for many years; some are new to their positions. Some have been at their current institutions for a long time; others are newly appointed. Most have had leadership roles in ACPA: College Student Educators International and/or NASPA: Student Affairs Professionals in Higher Education and/or several of the community college-focused associations.

## Data Analysis

The e-mail responses generated about 40 single-spaced pages of data, almost two-thirds of which—interestingly enough—focused on what troubled them. We analyzed the data as individuals and as a team, seeking commonalities and differences across the responses within each of the broad questions we asked: "What troubles you? What keeps you up at night?" and "What excites you? What keeps you going?" We generated six themes within each of the questions, although we recognize they are not wholly self-contained; they are related, shaping one another in complicated ways that might differ by campus. So, for example, access to success is likely to be inextricably linked to campus climates for diversity and inclusion, as well as students' health and well-being. With that caveat in mind, we offer the themes:

## Themes: What Troubles You? What Keeps You up at Night?

1. Affordability and access (including affordability of higher education to students and families; access to success, not just admission; access to high-quality and high-impact learning experiences; gaps in achievement and attainment).
2. Student health and well-being (including mental health challenges and services, campus and student safety, and campus resources to support student health and wellness)
3. Diversity and inclusion (including cultures and climates for diversity and inclusion, inclusive communities, concerns and demands regarding civility, free speech, and discourse of differences; student activism regarding inclusion; multiple and intersecting identities)
4. Regulations and compliance (including discourse about the value of higher education; external mandates, regulations, and political agendas; perceived conflicts between regulations and compliance and learning and education)
5. Technology and media (including influences on campuses of 24-hr news cycle and social media; climates of crisis, urgency, and instant gratification)
6. Student affairs (including roles, perceptions of competence, preparation and experiences, effectiveness of student affairs leadership, models of organization and practice, use of evidence and data to inform decisions)

Most of the responses to "What troubles you?" were framed by concerns about resources; that is, these issues were troubling, in part because of limited and declining financial and human resources. Therefore, instead of treating resources as a separate theme, we have discussed it in the text of the sourcebook as a critical context for what troubles the respondents.

## Themes: What Excites You? What Keeps You Going?

1. Students (including students as the center of the work, facilitating student learning and success, spending time with students, learning from students)
2. Making a difference (including the transformative powers of education, creating and sustaining inclusive communities, promoting social justice and equity, uses of digital technologies and social media)
3. Collaboration and community (including partnerships on and off campus, teamwork, extending campus borders, professional and civic engagement)
4. Leading and facilitating change (including institutional change and effectiveness, creating transformative organizations, engaging with the academic mission to create seamless learning environments,

contributions of student affairs to institutional effectiveness, leading change)
5. Learning, data, and scholarship (including being a learner; outcomes assessment and program evaluation; using data, theories, and scholarship for decision making; staying current)
6. "I love my job": Ultimately, it's all about *all* the work (including joy, hope, core values and principles, the whole of "what keeps me going")

These 12 themes form the basis for the discussions of data in Chapters 2 and 3 of this sourcebook. Not all of the data from the respondents are included in the themes, but we believe they encompass most of the data and reflect the priorities of the respondents. We did not, however, check the themes with the respondents prior to writing about the data in sourcebook; we did share the information with them as the sourcebook was being prepared. We have provided the responses verbatim (with identifying information removed) in Appendix C and Appendix D, so readers may, if they choose, consider the accuracy and credibility of our themes.

We also looked at the data across the two questions, seeking what appeared to be consistencies and contradictions; we addressed those issues in this issue, as well.

## Limitations

We recognize limitations in the data and our results, based on the sample and our data collection methods. For example, the data we received provided only snapshots of the respondents' experiences at the moment they answered our e-mail request. Had they chosen to reply at another time—another day or earlier or later in the same day—different experiences might have been troubling or exciting. For instance, during the month or so in Fall 2015 we sought responses from the leaders, several well-publicized incidents of campus violence occurred; some respondents who contacted us after those incidents mentioned them, but those from whom we heard before did not.

The data also cannot be interpreted to reflect or account for institutional or geographic characteristics or differences, although, as we noted above, we sought some variety in both. Unfortunately, about half of the 18 nonrespondents were senior leaders at private colleges and universities, so it could be argued that our data do not reflect the experiences of student affairs at those institutions adequately. In addition, our respondents were not just senior leaders in terms of organizational responsibilities, but they also could be considered "senior" in age—in most cases, over 50 year of age. We do not know what impact that might have had on the data they provided.

What we do know is we are grateful for the rich and thought-provoking information they shared with us, and we hope they consider our analyses and sense-making of that information to be credible and useful.

# Appendix B

**Respondents**

Kevin Banks, Vice President for Student Affairs, Morgan State University (MD)
Victor Boschini, Chancellor, Texas Christian University
Marilee Bresciani, Professor, San Diego State University
Susie Brubaker-Cole, Vice Provost for Student Affairs, Oregon State University
Jill E. Carnaghi, Assistant Vice President for Student Development, Saint Louis University
Karla Carney-Hall, Vice President for Student Affairs, Illinois Wesleyan University
Mary Coburn, Vice President for Student Affairs, Florida State University
Karen Warren Coleman, Vice President for Campus Life and Student Services, University of Chicago
Les Cook, Vice President for Student Affairs and Advancement, Michigan Technological University
Zebulun Davenport, Vice Chancellor Division of Student Affairs, Indiana University–Purdue University Indianapolis
Maggie de la Teja, Vice President for Student Development Services, Tarrant County College District (TX)
Gary Dukes, Vice President for Student Affairs, Western Oregon University
Wendy Endress, Vice President for Student Affairs, The Evergreen State University (WA)
Marsha Guenzler-Stevens, Director, Stamp Union, University of Maryland College Park
Gavin Henning, Associate Professor, New England College (NH)
John Hernandez, Vice President of Student Services, Santiago Canyon College (CA)
Luoluo Hong, Vice President for Student Affairs, San Francisco State University
Keith Howard, Vice President for Student Affairs, Colorado Community College System
Jillian Kinzie, Associate Director, Center for Postsecondary Research and NSSE Institute, Indiana University; Research Associate, National Institute for Learning Outcomes Assessment
Kevin Kruger, President, NASPA: Student Affairs Professionals in Higher Education
George Kuh, Director, National Institute for Learning Outcomes Assessment, and Chancellor's Professor Emeritus, Indiana University
Donna Lee, Vice President for Student Affairs, Macalester College

Susan Longerbeam, Associate Professor, Northern Arizona University
Cindi Love, Executive Director, ACPA: College Student Educators International
Patrick Love, Vice President of Student Affairs, New York Institute of Technology
Bill McDonald, Dean of Students, University of Georgia
Jason Meriwether, Vice Chancellor for Enrollment Management and Student Affairs, Indiana University Southeast
Shana Meyer, Vice President for Student Affairs, Missouri Western State University
Thomas Miller, Vice President for Student Affairs, University of South Florida
Larry Moneta, Vice President for Student Affairs, Duke University (NC)
Charles Nies, Interim Vice Chancellor for Student Affairs, University of California, Merced
Todd Olson, Vice President for Student Affairs and Dean of Students, Georgetown University
Anna Ortiz, Professor, California State University Long Beach
Patricia A. Perillo, Vice President for Student Affairs, Virginia Polytechnic Institute and State University
Scott Peska, Dean of Students, Waubonsee Community College (IL)
M. L. "Cissy" Petty, Vice President for Student Affairs, Loyola University New Orleans
Tim Pierson, Vice President for Student Affairs, Longwood University (VA)
Kent Porterfield, Vice President for Student Development, Saint Louis University
Jerry Price, Dean of Students, Chapman University (CA)
Kris Renn, Professor and Associate Dean of Undergraduate Studies, Michigan State University
Tom Rocklin, Vice President for Student Life, University of Iowa
Larry Roper, Professor, Oregon State University
John Schuh, Distinguished Professor Emeritus, Iowa State University
Robert Schwartz, Professor, Florida State University
Mike Segawa, Dean of Students, University of Puget Sound (WA)
Mahauganee Shaw, Assistant Professor, Miami University (OH)
Barbara Snyder, Vice President for Student Affairs, University of Utah
Annie Stevens, Vice Provost for Student Affairs, University of Vermont
Kurt Stimeling, Vice President for Student Affairs, Rivier University (NH)
Sherry Watt, Associate Professor, University of Iowa
Lori White, Vice Chancellor for Students, Washington University, Saint Louis
Patricia Whitely, Vice President for Student Affairs, University of Miami
Case Willoughby, Vice President for Student Services, Butler County Community College (KS)

# Appendix C

## What Troubles You? Another Way to Think About It: What Keeps You up at Night?

The following responses are verbatim; however, minor editing was done because of space limitations in the sourcebook. The responses are in random order, with all identifying information removed.

### Respondent 1 (R1)

- Role/perceptions/competence of student affairs: Disruption is the "norm" and those who have a clear story/narrative about what they do, how they contribute and who can tell this story/narrative in the language of the academy while translating it to regulators and legislators, parents and students will thrive. Student affairs does not have a clear and understandable narrative. We do not connect our work directly to recruitment/enrollment, persistence/retention nor completion.
- Evidence and data: We do not tell our stories well. We have not been effective in creating a compelling evidence-based narrative.

### R2

- Affordability that limits access and persistence.
- Safety: physical and interpersonal violence on campus.
- Questions about value of HE: public discourse regarding the value of higher education (is it worth it?) impact on public policy and legislation.
- Student health: legalizing marijuana without awareness of what this will mean for our society and social attitudes and behaviors of young people.

**R3.** Legal implications of campus safety: I could end up in a defendant's seat simply due to the behaviors of a student. The many forms could be: suicide, alcohol/drug abuse, sexual/domestic/interpersonal violence, etc. As a university, we can educate and enact many proactive programs/interventions/peer support, but the bottom line is that we will always miss someone who critically needed to hear the message.

### R4

- Safety: issues of campus safety and emergency preparedness on our campuses. We seem more content to continue operating from reactive protocols and procedures.

- Need to use evidence and data: neglect to use assessment and research data/findings in combination with strategic planning skills to direct our efforts and improve our practice.
- Inclusion and climates for difference: pervasive alienation and hostility that continue to taint the experiences of students, staff, and faculty with nondominant and marginalized identities.

### R5

- Student affairs preparation: We continue to train students for traditional student affairs units when the student population and institutions are dramatically changing.
- Future of private HE: I worry about all those small private colleges that are going to continue to decline in enrollment—how will they survive?

### R6

- Affordability: I worry about the affordability issue, especially for small privates, which by every measure I know of provide a better educational experience for undergrads.
- Access—quality experiences: I worry that the students who can most benefit from high-impact educational practices and similar enriching educational experiences are less likely to find their way into them.
- Federal regulation, compliance, interventions: I worry that the federal government may try to replace the current accreditation system with something far more dysfunctional.
- Data and evidence and corporate assessment: I worry that the big testing industry is going to corner the market on outcomes assessment tools that offer little guidance to faculty and staff for how the results/scores from these tools for improvement.
- Communication relearning out of class: I worry that we are still struggling to codify, capture, and articulate the powerful learning that occurs outside the classroom in conversations about the value of college (but the extended educational report that ACCRAO and NASPA are working on has promise in this regard).
- Student learning—away from holism: shift away from focus on [w]holistic education: I worry that the value of the associate and baccalaureate degrees may be compromised with the movement toward stackable credentials wherein badges and certificates will be counted or represented (in lieu of whatever is supposed to happen [in] college) in some yet to be determined way in those degrees. I worry that the segment of the age cohort who ought to get the "good stuff" (a healthy dose of liberal education) are being tracked into narrow skills preparation programs leading to certificates and badges, thus perpetuating and exacerbating the economic and social divides that characterize the nation today.

- Impact of technology on quality of student experiences: I worry that technology, no matter how sophisticated, will not replace a caring faculty or staff member who advocates on behalf of a student (thousands of them across the country on any given day) and turns a disappointment into an opportunity to excel.

**R7**

- Campus safety issues as an urban institution in Baltimore, MD! We are subject to random acts of crimes being perpetrated against our students!
- Access—financial aid to support our students.
- Federal regulation and compliance: Title IX issues.
- Student health: mental health issues.
- Personnel issues.

**R8**

- Putting out fires/climate of continuous crisis and immediate response: the constant need/attention toward "putting out fires"—student crises, media response, student conduct issues, staff performance concerns, budget reductions—and yet, this is where others (senior leaders, faculty, staff, etc.) value my role the most.
- Student health: addressing basic issues of health for our students—alcohol and other drug misuse and abuse, mental health concerns, violence, etc.
- Impact of external expectations—politics, regulation—access, affordability, compliance and the legal landscape, student safety, guaranteed outcomes, immediate communication.
- Impact of internal expectations, enrollment management, declining resources—enrollment numbers, retention rates, graduation rates, national benchmarking all within continual budget constraints.
- Questions about value of higher education, role of student affairs: lack of articulation about what makes higher education on a college campus and the field of student affairs relevant in the 21st century.
- Inclusion, diversity, role of student affairs: student affairs carrying the mission and values of diversity and social justice for the campus without much support or similar efforts in other parts of the university.
- Impact of technology: use and misuse of technology coupled with the need to stay current.

**R9**

- Campus safety, student health: Issues of campus safety and student well-being are a concern for me. Gun issues are a real threat, and particularly when coupled with the trend of mental health challenges that

today's college students are presenting in increasingly larger numbers. And even at [my institution], with a relatively "well off" student demographic, we are seeing more homelessness, hunger, and financial crisis than previously.
- Federal regulations, compliance, intervention, political pressures, declining resources: The challenges of enforcing Title IX and VAWA requirements (and really this whole era of increased government regulation and legal compliance) also concern me. I am not convinced that any of this is actually reducing the frequency of sexual violence on our campuses or otherwise increasing the well-being of the students, and the strain on already stretched resources is obvious. The issues that these regulatory laws are trying to address are real and they do require our serious attention, but I do not believe that increased government regulation is the answer. We do need better prevention and education strategies and real behavioral change, particularly among men, but response protocols do very little to help with this.
- Increasing complexity of "old issues": I agree that we have not made great strides in addressing old problems like substance abuse, sexual misconduct, campus civility issues, or the achievement gap. Today, the problems seem more multifaceted and layered.
- Students as consumers, role of parents: This is the age of college consumerism, where parents and students seem to want to be able to decide what they will or will not do, even when these choices interfere with curriculum, co-curriculum, or university policies that have been developed to enhance their learning, development and overall success.
- Resiliency: I worry as well about student resiliency, and I believe I may also be seeing less resiliency in new student affairs professionals.
- Impact of technology—24-hour news cycle and nonstop social media (simple portrayals of complex situations); climate of crisis; speed of change and response: The 24-hour news cycle and the reality of nonstop social media has not only changed how students interact but also changed the way activism happens on our campuses and in society. Things move at warp speed today, offering student affairs professionals and other campus officials very little time to think and respond. It's not the activism that concerns me, rather it is the way the media covers activism and the pressures that are then placed on our work as a consequence.
- Student affairs competence—old models; inclusion and diversity: As our campuses become increasingly more diverse in every way, I worry that our current models of practice were designed for another time. Developing models of practice (and even organizational structures) for homogeneous student populations is much easier than designing approaches for increasingly heterogeneous populations. As new learning and student development theories have emerged from research about historically underrepresented students in higher education over the last decade or so,

new programs and models of practice have been developed, but they have largely been "additive" to what student affairs is already doing. Given the current and future economics of higher education, this seems unsustainable. A better approach, or so it seems to me, is to rethink what we are doing and retool what we have. In terms of student success, many of our practice models are "industrial" or group oriented, but students' needs seem to be increasingly more individualistic (think intersectionality). I believe this requires a different approach, and I do worry about whether we have the stomach for this type of dramatic shift in our field.

### R10

- Student health, resiliency, enforcement: Many of our students carry heavy individual burdens that affect their behaviors and performance on a university campus. How do we weigh their personal situations versus the needs of other students on campus?
- Climate of crisis and immediate response; safety: None of us ever knows when everything might need to be dropped to work on a student or campus emergency. Students face some big challenges.... sometimes it is difficult to see the tough times students are going through.

**R11.** Increasing complexity of "old issues": The concerns, issues, challenges that were prevalent in the late 1970s and 1980s are still around, but only more intense, complex, troubling, divisive, and litigious: alcohol use and abuse, combination of alcohol and other drugs, sexual misconduct, sorority and fraternity ideals and realities, civility or lack thereof, intersectionalities of identities, definitions of "family" and what constitutes a family (multiple marriages and partners and siblings from different parents), level of academic readiness and preparedness, the greater divide or disparity between the haves and have nots, students not even considering themselves as "adults" and parental intervention—even over meal plans and some of the more mundane aspects of attending college, technology and social media and always being plugged in and multitasking—rarely fully present, teaching versus learning paradigm, engagement of students in meaningful conversations, resiliency (or lack of) and everyone gets a ribbon or medal for showing up ...

### R12

- Federal regulations, compliance, intervention: concerns about how we deal with all of the compliance issues being thrown at institutions with little increase in support to add positions or responsibilities to accommodate new mandates.

- Impact of technology, pace of change: the rapid pace of advances in technology and the inability to keep up both in terms of training and adoption of new practices.
- Institutional leadership: a president retiring in the near future and wonder about who will succeed him.
- Enrollment management: being able to continue our enrollment growth with decreasing numbers of high school graduates.
- Fraternities: the age-old issue of fraternity struggles and unwillingness of national organizations to work with institutions and hold chapters accountable.

### R13

- Scarce/declining resources, climate of crisis: What's keeping me up at night was exactly what caused me to be late in responding to you. For the last 6 months the university has been working in a presidential advisory group on the university's financial equilibrium. Although this isn't new news ... it seems more potent when you are smack in the middle of it all. We have a [significant] deficit to close and it means both programs and people will be discontinued and dismissed. We have a window of 5 years to get this right, and I believe we will but it won't be without an emotional cost to many.
- Enrollment management: I have learned a great deal about folks' resilience in the last few months and am impressed with the due diligence around the table. I am grateful for the BOT's support, but the reality is we need to be "right sized" given an enrollment downfall 2 years ago.

### R14

- Federal compliance issues (Title IX issues).
- Student safety/death—school shootings

### R15

- Safety and impact of safety concerns on learning environments/learning: After [a campus] shooting last week, I will add what troubles me is an erosion of learning environments. In particular, I am troubled by deleterious effect on learning and development caused by generalized fears for physical safety.
- Value of HE, scarce/declining resources: declining public and legislative support for and criticism of institutions that support the public good. Higher education institutions are centered in the trend toward declining support and increasing criticism of the public commons.
- Discourse re students, inclusion and diversity: related to the item above, criticism that conflates students (and their parents). Articles that claim

knowledge of entire generations (millennials), using reductionist terms (entitled, unprepared, helicopter, lacking resilience). Generalized characterizations disregard cultural and socioeconomic diversity, distort the truth and neglect the tremendous talent and agency of college students.

**R16**

- Student affairs organizations/perceptions revalue: after decades of research and well established best practices about how students succeed and learn, that our institutions continue to dissect the student experience and box it within our existing silos and organizational structures. That learning within the classroom continues to "trump" learning beyond the classroom in ways that minimizes and does not validate our work and our roles. In this day and age, many student affairs divisions and/or professionals are still justifying their existence or need for adequate funding.
- Higher ed organizations, structures of "elitism": the elitism engrained in the academy that creates and maintains a "class" system depending on the role you have on a college campus (faculty [tenured, adjunct, non-teaching faculty], administration, staff); type of institution you work at (research, public land grant, two-year or vocational college, etc.); your discipline or department (humanities vs. natural sciences, career technical education vs. liberal arts); and our divisional structures (academic affairs, student affairs, administrative services, etc.).
- Politics intruding in HE, declining resources: state legislatures that are politicizing our educational institutions regardless of the political direction (left or right). Wisconsin is an example of efforts to dissolve collective bargaining, tenure, etc., and California is an example where the legislature (in our economic upswing) is allocating millions of dollars to community colleges in areas of student success and student equity. While these resources are needed and welcomed for our work to be effective, there are unrealistic expectations for immediate gains—with repercussions if we can't deliver fast enough.
- Preparation of SSAOs, qualifications, expectations; SA leadership: increased expectations and skills for SSAOs (for which few of us have been trained or prepared for), including development/fundraising; enrollment management; construction management/development of new facilities; developing external partnerships; risk management, etc. Implication creates opportunities to meet specific and unique professional development needs of SSAOs.
- Inclusion and diversity, institutional leadership: institutions with diverse student demographics but that lack equal representation among their ranks of administrators and faculty (especially faculty). Well established processes and protocols (and attitudes) that when dissected and analyzed are nothing short of covert examples and/or a history of institutional racism.

### R17

- Resources—scarce, declining: Every indication is that appropriations and tuition will struggle to even keep up with inflation for as far as I can see. How can we generate new revenues or reduce expenses?
- Student activism: We're seeing a minor resurgence, which I welcome, but I want us to be good at responding.
- Federal regulations and compliance, Title IX; student safety: compliance in general, and reducing gender-based violence. 'Nuff said.
- Black student success. Our student success efforts have been effective for all groups except black students. I [created] a new position to devote to this.
- Institutional governance and leadership.

### R18

- Personnel decisions—these range from dismissing someone to dealing with the on-going drama of otherwise solid staff members.
- Campus safety: threat assessment situations involving mostly students and an increasing number that involves faculty and staff.
- Fed regs and compliance, Title IX—those matters of a serious nature and our comprehensive response to all parties that must be knit together in ways, at times, are simply overly and unnecessarily complex. Volume of new legislation in the midst of implementing current policy changes.
- Student health and safety, emergencies: psychological emergencies—the increase and complexity of cases, the volume referred to the Care Team, and expenditure of staff resources on this population.
- Decline in student and staff resiliency—the drain on staff and faculty with matters that are a student's responsibility. Likewise, this issue of low-resiliency is a trait of new professionals—passionate about their own dreams without making the bigger connection, leaving in the middle of the semester, lack of commitment to make a lasting contribution to the institution, which cannot be accomplished in 2 years or less.

### R19

- Resources—scarce, declining; politics, fed and state support: I am very worried about the economic realities that we face in the next decade. I think at last count there are eight or nine governors who have put sweeping budget reductions to higher ed on the table. With the public pressure to keep tuition down, the fact that we are at record tuition discounting rates nationwide, and that we will likely see further erosion of state support of higher ed, I think we are looking at some very tough times ahead. Student affairs as well as all full-time faculty and many academic departments will be facing budget challenges. I think, we will be looking at a

contraction in student affairs over this next decade. It hasn't happened yet—but it seems inevitable.
- Student affairs roles, organizations, leadership, models of practice: which relates to an opportunity I think for all of student affair[s]? How do we re-engineer, reorganize, merge, and cut to realize efficiencies? I have a thought about this, which I have been testing in the speeches I give—that is the idea that the age of specialization may and should come to an end in student affairs. We have seen significant specialization over the past 25 years, more services, more experts, more departments. I wonder if we need to begin thinking about a return to more generalists—student affairs staff that have broader sets of responsibilities. Community colleges have already moved to this model. I think it is interesting to wonder whether student affairs is adaptive and flexible enough to broaden our influence and impact to student[s] who are not first-time, full-time, largely residential students. What is our role with students who may be completing some or all of their coursework online? What is our role with posttraditional students? Our history is based on the traditional student—how can we pivot to expand our role with the fastest-growing segment in higher education?
- Student learning and attainment, changing student characteristics, access and affordability: The attainment gap issues that result in low completion rates for low-income [students], first-generation [students], and students of color is a national disgrace. I see this as the most compelling issue of our time and think we are generally unprepared for the waves of new students coming to our campuses in the next 10 years. I think it will be quite a challenge—for we actually know a lot about attainment for these new students—but it is expensive and staff intensive. The question will be then, how do we scale these existing boutique programs to serve an ever larger group of low-income students who will be coming to our campuses? All in a time of constrained resources.
- Impact of technology: Related to the above—can we see real progress in student affairs developing technologically mediated interactions with students that get at community, engagement, intentional learning, etc.? So far little progress, but I am hopeful, the technology competency may result in some progress here.

**R20**

- Role of student affairs, student learning and attainment: My concern is that [student] affairs is not sufficiently involved in issues of educational quality, student success, and the broader spectrum of student learning outcomes on most campuses. As we know, student affairs educators have a lot to contribute, but they don't seem to have found their way into relevant conversations if this is happening on campuses, or aren't in good positions to lead the discussion if others aren't taking them up on campus.

- Impact—fed regulations and compliance, campus safety, student health, crisis climate, setting priorities for student success: When I talk with student affairs leaders, many are overwhelmed with issues of compliance, troubled students, problem issues on campus, including athletics, sexual assault, integrity ... and have trouble allocating time to bigger student success issues, or they are working in an environment where there is little expectation for them to be involved in issues of student success or educational quality.
- So, pretty general but I wanted to get the concern for student learning and success in there!

### R21

- Student health [and] student drug use.
- Compliance and regs versus student learning and success: less time spent educating and more time complying or preventing litigation; serving most students well versus a few extremely well.
- Student affairs organizations, staff roles, scarce resources: staff turnover and competency/enthusiasm for the work in 2015+.
- Discourse [about the] value of higher education: the value/lack thereof of higher education in the US.

### R22

- Student safety and loss of life: If my phone rings after midnight, I am always afraid that a student has passed away in an accident, a suicide, or some other unexpected way. My biggest fear is a student suicide by someone who didn't get help with their challenges through counseling, and that we never got a chance to help them. We work assiduously to advertise and share our counseling and support service, and my fear is that someone will not respond and we lose them before we can try to help. Even though this is something I cannot control, I worry about this.
- Fraternities: My second concern in this area is hazing. I have seen students hurt before due to senseless violence. Although I am comfortable we have had the appropriate training and the University is "covered" in terms of due diligence and issues of reasonable foresight, losing a life that way is so frightening.

### R23

- Student safety, campus violence: school and campus shootings: The recent FBI report indicates that they are happening at a frequency about one per month. Today, there is a mass shooting at Umpqua Community College. A little over 2 weeks ago there was a shooting at Delta State University. The concern I have is that we are teaching our young to prepare

for active shooter scenarios in K–12 and yet, much of higher education we do not adequately teach people to respond to these violent intruders.
- Furthermore, I think we have more responsibility to help educate today's youth about the responsibility to "advocate" for change legislatively to enact stronger laws that could reduce this violence. Most mass shootings the guns are purchased legally or students take them from their home or relative's homes.

### R24

- Higher education change, data, adapting to scarcer resources; new organizational models: The tension between perceptions that higher education is becoming too much like a business and losing its core values and the opportunity for higher ed to learn from the business sector about how to scale up services, utilize predictive analytics, and work toward key performance indicators. I tend to think that higher ed does have a lot to learn from the business world and hope that we can get past the stigma attached to adopting (and adapting) practices from that realm to meet our own, very different goals.
- Student affairs staff, responsiveness to change: helping staff to adapt to change and creating enthusiasm for longstanding staff who are more senior in their careers to embrace new practices and approaches to our educational practices.
- Scarce and declining resources, unfunded mandates, more with less: resource[s], resources, resources. We operate on a very thin budget, but are under improvement mandate. How does that add up?
- Fed regs and compliance: fear of falling short on a major compliance issue and consequences of doing so: fines, institutional reputation, personal reputation, and professional viability.

### R25

- Inclusion and diversity: the surface-level approaches to addressing diversity/difference.
- Institutional leadership: the misuse of power by administrators.

### R26

- Student affairs preparation, leadership; impact of technology: I often wonder how long it will be before we experience a significant decline in enrollment in our programs. Our master's degree is still very robust and energized with new students. Doc students is a challenge. More and more it is the case that people pursuing a doctoral degree do not or cannot take an "oath of poverty", and sell or rent their house and move to a research university for 4 (or more) years to get a doctoral degree (as we did many years ago). The majority these days seem to want it delivered on their

desktop, laptop, or similar device, and if they come to campus, want to do it for a few days only. They want to do it while they keep their full-time job and are scared or at least unwilling to leave a job, family, home, etc. to take the "risk" of adding another degree. Master's folks have "little to lose and much to gain" from a 2-year master's program so they are glad to come to campus.
- I am not sure what difference, if any, the move to "on-line doctoral education" may make in quality or even connections between colleagues in the future. Are on-line doctoral degrees going to be the same experience? No, but will the quality be comparable? Maybe. We are going in that direction but I don't know what it will mean.

**R27.** Inclusion and diversity, student attainment, access and success: What troubles me are all of the persons underrepresented in higher education who will experience few, if any, of the perks of the "American Dream" during a lifetime. Our world suffers, therefore.

**R28.** Funding models, declining resources: The major problem that I see is the long-term funding not only for student affairs but also for higher education in general. So much in the way of paying for college is placed on the backs of students as states and parents back away from providing support for college students. I am not sure where this will head but it is clear that the current trends are not sustainable. In [my state], in particular, there is very little talk (other than 529 plans) of parents assisting or paying for their students' education. That is so different than my experience, when the norm was that parents would help to a great extent.

**R29.** Student health (mental health): the increasingly larger number of students who come to campus with serious mental health issues—many that are not addressed by their families—many that are addressed. Often times they are really not prepared to enter the campus environment.

**R30**

- Resilience, mental health: The fragility of today's student … lack of resilience … lack of coping skills … high anxiety … to the point that I worry about the students who are falling through the cracks because they are not on "high alert" … the student who may just need a little extra nudge and support, but is not in crisis.
- Climate of crisis versus education: Our role as educators is becoming harder to stand in as we continue to need hone our skills as crisis managers.

**R31**

- Student affairs leadership, student affairs preparation, student affairs roles: profession that is led by vice presidents for student affairs (VPSAs)

who either do not know the scholarship of learning and human development or don't know how to apply it or don't know how to lead in a learning-centered way. I am also concerned that more and more VPSAs are hired without a background or training in student affairs or higher education. The lack of intercultural competency that dominates the profession and higher education associations.
- Discourse about value of higher ed: I am deeply concerned about the lack of public trust for higher education and the lack of understanding of how education is the only hope for a more equitable and just future.
- Declining resources: The continued lack of federal and state funding for higher education is forcing campuses to act out of places of "survival" versus places of thoughtful consideration for its future.
- Fed and state regs, compliance, unfunded mandates: Federal and state mandates, particularly related to issues of Title IX, have the significant possibility of affecting the positive ways we can do this important work.
- Inclusion and diversity, inequities, campus climates: gender, racial, and other social identity inequities in an industry that professes otherwise.

### R32

- Climate of crisis, immediacy, urgency; impact of technology: how urgent everything is these days – everyone wants instant response, instant action. The media, our students, their parents all want instant gratification. (Can you tell my button is pushed?)
- Campus safety: Beyond that knee-jerk reaction though, what keeps me awake is safety. It seems like our world, what students are exposed to, and the risks that they often take have escalated. I don't feel that I can assure parents that their sons/daughters will be safe in college. I feel that as institutions we are doing more than ever to educate them about risks and reduce violence but it is still a major challenge. These risks have always been present; the degree just seems higher to me now.

### R33

- Roles of student affairs, shifts from education to compliance, external policy mandates, fears of litigation: One of the things that troubles me is that we are losing good people due to the seismic changes happening in the profession. [Former colleague] wrote a great piece on this as she departed the field. It began 35 years ago with the change in the drinking age that shifted our focus from teaching students about responsible consumption and being able to keep discipline related to alcohol-related behaviors rather than merely having alcohol. Then there were the external entities who took exception to a focus on building inclusive communities and challenging incoming students' perspectives on differences.

- The blunt-edged policy mandates that we all now face is a continual and evolving challenge. I now rarely return a phone call to a parent without checking with legal counsel first. So much time is spent responding to a multiplicity of external entities. And I am on a campus without a football team, without a traditional Greek system, and with a small on-campus population. Maybe that's why these other things bother me more!

**R34.** Campus safety, risky student behaviors, impact of technology: As hard as we try to educate students about "sex, drugs, and rock and roll" it just takes one incident to become a campus crisis and a media firestorm with fingers pointed back at us for what we did not do well.

**R35.** Fed regs and compliance, Title IX versus student learning, development, education: It's not that I am reluctant to take on high expectations for our response to sexual harassment/assault; it's that the DOE OCR [Department of Education] [Office of Civil Rights] has dictated so many aspects of how we respond. While well-intentioned (I'm giving them the benefit of the doubt), their efforts have shifted the institutional response to one led by caring student affairs professionals to one being managed by attorneys—both for the students and the institution. As hard as I have fought to retain a student development approach, our Title IX process is becoming less and less an educational process and more of a legal/criminal one. The saddest part is that these are situations in which students need our expertise the most, and we are increasingly denied the opportunity to do what we do best.

### R36

- Title IX and our focus on compliance-related matters/response to OCR rather than transformational education and dialogue.
- Resilience: "Fragility" and/or lack of resilience in students: this is real—how did we get here and how do we support these students in productive and meaningful ways?
- Support for low-income students: How are we really supporting poor students in highly selective institutions? Financial support is key—but it is not the only factor.
- Diversity and inclusion, civility, free speech: balancing free expression with (diversity and) inclusion—these needn't be incongruent, but often collide.
- Student behavior: increase in time-consuming aberrant student behavior situations and frequent interest by impacted parties (fellow students, impacted faculty/staff) that we "do something about it" [regardless of whether the behavior is actionable].
- 24-hour news/social media cycle, simplicity versus complexity is often misleading, reckless—and medium is not good for messaging complex issues.

## R37

- Student affairs leadership, roles, expectations, preparation: that our profession (read: SSAO pipeline)—and higher education executive leadership in general—is not attracting the best and the brightest but is instead oftentimes the "back up pathway" for those who either did not have the competency or the tenacity to pursue a "first choice" profession, while conversely, those with the passion and excellence needed for student affairs or other higher education executive leadership roles are not choosing this as a pathway; on a related note, the rubrics (both explicit and implicit) we use for selecting our leaders are oftentimes irrelevant or incomplete.
- Regs and compliance versus leadership and education: that the increasing administrative and compliance burdens generated by state and federal legislatures, as well as external regulatory entities, such as accreditation bodies, are diverting us away from transformational leadership by keeping us occupied with management of transactional tasks.
- Access, attainment, low income students—gaps: that despite breaking gender and racial barriers to promote increased access *in concept* to higher education, the access and achievement gap between those in the lowest income quartile and those in the highest income quartile is increasing rather than decreasing *in reality*.
- Competition for declining resources—managing behavior versus educating, competing roles and expectations for HE: that growing pressures to become social welfare agencies (responding to mental health issues, sexual violence/sexual misconduct, etc.) draws away personnel, fiscal, and time resources away from our educational and learning missions—that the unthoughtful, unpurposeful proliferation of technology creates the illusion of increased productivity and improved access, when in fact it generates a whole array of new problems for which we don't have the innovation or creative skills to fully respond to in a proactive manner.
- Accountability: that we are rapidly escalating the costs of higher education, but have not developed ways to critically self-reflect, self-monitor or hold ourselves accountable for responsible investment of tuition and other funding to respond to prioritized student needs; i.e., it continues to cost more to deliver the same instruction and student services without demonstrated value added. That intention continues to be privileged over impact, and that administrators do far more decision-making than delivering on desired outcomes.

## R38

- Organizational models, resistance to change, and holistic focus on student success: resistance to adopting new ways of working that TRULY

cross organizational boundaries to focus on holistic student success (academic, personal, social, spiritual, etc.).
- Student affairs competence: bad behavior by student and academic affairs midlevel professionals—backbiting/stabbing, sabotage, schadenfreude, "phoning it in" instead of bringing their whole selves. Even worse when it comes from senior folks ... but I'm learning that the midlevel attitude can crush the spirit of new professionals and mute the effect of anything new coming from senior level.

**R39.** Highest on my list of concerns for our profession is more of a higher education issue not just a student affairs challenge: access and affordability. We in American higher education know how to best educate students ... but we have not figured out in the 4-year setting how to deliver that affordably to all students who seek it. Those of us who work in the small college setting are able to utilize many if not all of those effective educational practices but we have a sticker cost of $60,000/year. In the large university setting, we are relatively cheaper but do that through many large lecture hall pedagogy. This is a fundamentally flawed model that is not effectively addressing our societal challenge of socioeconomic/class disparity. It may actually be exacerbating it.

**R40.** Regs and compliance issues, particularly Title IX, VAWA, and Clery. Making sure that staff are trained, that we are providing the appropriate information and programming to students, so that OCR does not come knocking on the door.

**R41**

- Regs and compliance: increased regulatory burdens from all directions: Title IX through financial aid (gainful employment, etc.) that take a huge amount of time away from mission critical work.
- Roles, expectations, perceptions, contributions of student affairs: Our leading professional associations have not yet led us to a place at the policy table to discuss our current and potential contributions: student learning (leadership, cultural competencies) and success (think completion agenda). I think college presidents misunderstand our work and underestimate our potential. We must get in front of college presidents as a group so that they know what we are capable of. (this may scare some SSAOs who do not want to live up to increased expectations ...)

**R42**

- Student learning, success, and development; roles and expectations and competence of student affairs: The lack of awareness about how students learn and develop among student affairs professionals and the academy as a whole keeps me awake at night. To cite the wisdom of the *Student*

*Learning Imperative*, student learning and development are inextricably intertwined is true and is now being proven by emerging neuroscience research ...
- Student affairs organizations, models of practice: If student affairs professionals in particular don't begin to rethink the way they do their work and evaluate it—who exactly will be the ones who invite in a different conversation to the table about what the commodity of higher education actually is ...

**R43**

- Student health (mental health), resilience: complex mental health issues and the lack of coping skills students possess to solve their own problems.
- Affordability long term of higher education for first-generation students in particular.
- Student affairs preparation, expectations, competence: long-term skill set of new professionals in student affairs and their ability to succeed under rapidly declining resources.

**R44**

- Value and roles of higher education, holistic education, political pressures: I continue to be troubled by a focus of higher education as workforce preparation. This is particularly concerning in the current political climate with the reauthorization of the Higher Education Act looming near. While higher education does prepare students for careers, I think this perspective is short-sighted and places the emphasis on skills needed "now" in the workforce.
- The world is changing more rapidly than any other time in history and our future leaders need skills and knowledge to solve problems that haven't even occurred yet. I think, back to my graduate work in student affairs as an example. Very little of what I learned in 1991–1993 is applicable now. Assessment was not even in our vocabulary, yet I ended up building a career around it. In the past 22 years, I have had to develop new skills and acquire new knowledge. I think, if we can move the focus to higher education preparing individuals to be problem solvers and global citizens, they will be prepared for the workforce and to solve the emerging issues in society.

**R45.** Student health and well-being: What keeps me up at night continues to surround all those things that are related to student well-being: alcohol use and abuse; mental health (especially as it appears suicide rates are climbing); sexual misconduct (and, of course Title IX compliance), and increasingly, time spent away from campus and the risks associated with travel, international tensions and cultural differences.

**R46**

- Regulations and compliance, Title IX: sexual assault compliance requirements.
- Student health and well-being: mental health and campus safety/emergency response.
- Institutional leadership—preparation, changes: presidential transitions and the changing nature of that work (levels of experience, experience in higher ed, experience with liberal arts colleges) and how that impacts our work.
- Inclusion and diversity, campus climates: diversity climate and frustrations about work still to do.
- Access and affordability of private higher education funding/tuition models for private higher education.

**R47**

- Student health and well-being, resilience.
- Role of higher education—as social service agency.
- Declining resources: the growing proportion of troubled students. An increased need for counseling services. A generation that seems more privileged but less resilient than any previous college-going group. More homeless students. More hungry students. More students in poverty. More students in recovery and our decreasing ability to meet their needs.

**R48.** Role of higher education—social and economic inequities: the growing racial and economic divide in this country and how institutions of higher education can effectively lead the momentum for change.

**R49**

- Regulations, compliance; student health and well-being; declining resources: keeping up with Title IX changes. Handling ADA requests and the ballooning of therapy requests. Meeting medical and mental health demands without raising student health fees through the roof
- Affordability in environment of increasing needs and declining resources: generally how to keep college and services affordable to our first-generation and low-income students.

**R50**

- Student health and well-being: escalating mental health issues and the need to balance resources for short-term and long-term solutions.

- Value of higher education, public trust: public's declining respect and trust of integrity and utility of higher education.
- Government intrusion and/or imposed solutions without understanding the nature of the issues.
- Increasing expectations for facilities and services amid declining resources: ongoing recession and economic issues versus escalating costs of higher education, including arms race for facilities improvement and innovation.

### R51

- Student health and well-being, resilience: I worry we are not teaching young people resiliency.
- I worry that we are trying to solve all of their problems to keep them from harm or pain or discomfort when those very difficult moments would probably leave them lessons to last a lifetime.
- I worry about the fragility of students—and worry—will we be there when they need us?
- Impact of technology, social media: I worry that we have forgotten how to have face-to-face conversations. When students need to talk it out with their peers—they don't know how. That inability to seek support or advice or feedback leaves people isolated or ill informed.
- Focus on student learning: I worry that we care too much about efficiencies and revenue in higher education that we forgot that learning is our enterprise.
- Civility versus free speech: I worry that we are afraid of killing speech we don't like with more speech, so we want someone to squelch the speech for us.
- Expectations of faculty versus student learning and success: I worry young scholars are so worried about their own research and career trajectory that they have forgotten the value of investing in students as mentors and teachers.

### R52

- Student health and well-being, demands for resources as resources decline: Student mental health issues are growing more serious, and it is difficult to meet demands for clinical care, for "case management" services, and for outreach on these issues. While we have staffed up in several departments, we are still seeing increasing needs among our students.
- Regulations and compliance, Title IX, government intrusion and interference with core functions amid declining resources: The current pressure around sexual assault and Title IX compliance is intense, and constantly evolving. The issue is very real, and we need to take it seriously. With that noted, the governmental activism—from many different fronts—is

frantic and has become unnecessarily intrusive into our work. We need to find an appropriate balance between the urgent need to focus on these issues, and the ability for institutions to develop and manage their own processes, policies, programs, and services.

**R53**

- Student health and well-being, demands for resources as resources decline: mental health issues of our students. The inability to keep up with the volume of students seeking mental health services is putting stress on the staff who are there to assist.
- Expectations for instant gratification and no personal responsibility: students' learned inability to accept personal responsibility. The expectations of immediacy and "do it for me" demands being placed on student affairs staff concerns me around their inability to take personal responsibility for their learning and their lives.
- Regulations and compliance, unfunded mandates amid shrinking resources: compulsory programs and services. The continued mandates to provide services that are being imposed on campuses by outside agencies is creating a backlog of unfunded mandates that will be required to offer at the expense of other programs.

# Appendix D

## What Excites You? Another Way to Think About It: What Keeps You Going?

The following responses are verbatim; however, minor editing was done because of space limitations in the sourcebook. The responses are in random order, with all identifying information removed.

### Respondent 1 (R1)

- Students keep me going. I came here to support them by supporting the professionals who support them. When I get discouraged, I make a campus visit.
- I love what I do because I am in the midst of that journey and get to experience the shifts in the lives of students. Social media gives us a tool with which to connect around the world, tell these stories and increase awareness about what students need. I am excited about this tool as a way to provide thought leadership, to amplify the voices of students and professionals, and to mobilize all of us to places of strength in our individual and collective work. I have developed five stories about students whom I have known and directly connected their experiences to the work of student affairs. We need 5 × 5,000.

### R2

- The continued power of education to transform lives.
- The growing diversity of our campuses and the potential that provides to provide global education.
- The strength of assessment efforts, which provides us with more data on students' needs, expectations, experiences and behaviors than ever before—we know more than ever.

**R3.** I'm continually amazed at the resiliency of the human spirit. Every year, I'm astounded when I learn of a student's journey to college. I think "how did they have the resolve to stick with [IT]?" (whatever "it" is). It could be a broken home, personal recovery from alcohol or drug abuse, poverty, mental illness, international travel, world crises, etc. Helping these students achieve their dream of a college education is truly a privilege.

**R4**

- My ability and drive to have a meaningful impact on the things that trouble me.
- The surfacing of faculty, student, and community activism that empowers people to push back on systemic injustices and creates avenues to make that possible.

**R5**

- I'm excited about working with first-generation college students and seeing the impact they have in bringing others in their family and communities into higher education.
- I also am excited about the opportunities student affairs has to engage in the academic mission of the university and work with faculty colleagues to make their classrooms the place for engagement—as they often are at urban, commuter institutions. We can help them create community in their classroom and to partner with them in the spaces and places these students "live" in the small amount of time they may be on campus.
- If (some would say when) there is a large-scale move to performance-based funding we are really going to have to show how we contribute to retention, graduation and time to degree—not just have a philosophical "belief" that we do based on our anecdotal experiences. These are real opportunities to change the way we think, the way we do our work, the ways we influence and create policy.

**R6.** No response.

**R7**

- Students who possess the grit to forge ahead despite their shortcomings.
- Visionary leadership.
- Colleagues who genuinely care about our students.
- Opportunities to work across divisions.
- Community engagement opportunities.

**R8**

- Mentorship/leadership—providing guidance and access to higher education for future students and young professionals.
- Collaboration and managing change—develop innovative programs and services in partnership with faculty, staff, and administrators.
- Advocacy—Serve as a voice for the student experience—and how we can positively impact college students.

- Partnership—with faculty, donors, researchers who can push us beyond the boundaries of our own student affairs world and support the student experience in new and different ways.

### R9

- As [others have] said in their responses, I am still motivated by the ideals that led me to choose this career path. I am energized by the many opportunities and challenges that are a part of student affairs work.
- I still love working with students although I believe the "millennial" generation is different in some significant ways to previous generations of students with whom I have worked.
- I believe in the transformative power of a college education, and I am excited about the possibility of educating more students from the marginalized communities of society. This, I believe, is the hope of our future as a nation and as a global society.
- I believe in concepts of inclusion and equity, and I sense that the tide in our country may be shifting.
- I still believe we can make a difference in the lives of our students; that has never changed for me. I have great optimism for the partnerships we are developing with our faculty and academic leaders.
- There seems to be a greater appreciation on my campus for what student affairs does, what contributions we make, and for what future we can co-create for our institution.
- I am excited about the broadening of our campus borders to include the community and the powerful learning that can take place through community and civic engagement.
- I also think the responsible use of digital technology and social media may be a good way for us to impact students on a larger scale, reaching those who heretofore may not have been able to access traditional student affairs programs and services.
- And I am also excited, albeit nervous, about the prospects of rethinking student affairs organizations and practice to align better with the critical objectives and outcomes that our institutions have for student learning, development and overall success. Despite the many, many challenges that confront U.S. higher education at this time, I believe our best days may be ahead of us.

### R10

- The excitement on a student's face when she overcomes an obstacle; the relieved tone in a parent's voice when a situation has been addressed; the student's self-reflection on how much he has grown in his time on campus; even the Code of Conduct respondent who claims responsibility for her part in a violation and learns from the situation.

- Thinking about my mentors and how I can carry the mentorship forward also keeps me going. I consider two of my past supervisors to be mentors. One leads from the heart and uses emotion, compassion, and personal relationship building in his leadership style. The other is a visionary who relies on others to complete the step-by-step processes and details to ensure his vision comes to fruition. Both took a personal interest in me and have invested themselves in helping me to succeed in the field, encouraging me and introducing me to others in the field and to new concepts. Knowing I can pay, it forward excites me and keeps me going.
- I like that my job varies from day to day. I am afforded the opportunity to lead groups; to complete detail-oriented reports; to connect with students; to work with and supervise a fantastic staff team; and to use creativity to address needs. It's also fun! I get to see amazing student productions, watch students grow as leaders and develop in their thought processes, work with fun people, and live the college life!

**R11.** Again, probably some of the same things that brought me into the field: students, student leaders, being part of a team, fostering a common vision/mission/goals/aspirations, new and younger professionals with all their idealism and commitment to making a difference, the coming together of the academic side of the house and student affairs to create a seamless living/learning environment for students, working with others to come up with better solutions/options/opportunities, ability to look "bigger" at the campus/institution and the ways to collaborate and more explicitly connect the dots for oneself/staff/students, outreach to the community and how the institution and the community relate and impact the larger community/common good, concept of global citizenship as well as "service" to and with others, ability to complicate our thinking in more interesting ways to look at current situations, problem solving . . . .

**R12**

- I have a dynamic structure that includes all of student affairs, enrollment management, athletics, advancement, alumni relations, and marketing/communications. This model affords us the opportunity to look at prospects/students/alums and others through a lifecycle of engagement. As a result, collaboration, communication, teamwork, and productivity are enhanced. It's great!
- Our students. I have never worked with such a bright, passionate, committed group as my students today.
- Nearly 400 companies at our career fair last week with 1,300 individual recruiters for our roughly 1,500 grads this year. A 96% placement rate and some of the highest starting salaries in the country.

- Having the largest number of female students ever in our first year class at 29% and making progress towards are overall goal of being 35% female by 2020.
- The prospect of advancing interests in mindfulness work and infusing more into our campus.
- Working with an incredible team of colleagues that constantly have top of mind awareness and thinking about student and alumni success.
- Surpassing our annual fundraising goal the last 2 years running since advancement moved under student affairs.
- Having a campus community/alumni and others that are fully passionate about making a difference.
- Being challenged every day, willing to take risks, have fun and enjoy what life brings.

**R13.** I leap from my bed every morning grateful to do this work—our work matters, has meaning, is both empathic and strategic.

**R14.** The scholarship aspect of our work and impact that we have on the total development of students

**R15**

- Students accessing higher education, in ever-greater numbers, from a rich array of cultural groups and life experiences. They bring resilience, humility, hunger for learning, and respect for wisdom. Students in colleges and universities today give me hope for the future of humanity.
- The use of technology in support of learning. A rapidly evolving understanding of learning, along with the rapidly evolving technology in support of human learning, gives me great hope for the future of learning and sustenance of our world.

**R16**

- While the national completion agenda and emphasis on clear pathways to graduation applies institutional pressures it should ensure a "place at the table" for student affairs as educational partners in these initiatives. Similarly, renewed focus on student learning and success provides unique opportunities to examine our institutional practices, policies, and priorities that should (emphasis on should) keep the focus where it should be: student learning and student success …
- Accreditation standards that require systematic and continuous planning, assessment, and evaluation (whether they be framed as program review, student learning outcomes, service area outcomes, etc.) all have one common denominator: to demonstrate how institutions monitor student achievement and student learning and how the results of these efforts drive planning, resource allocation, and program effectiveness …

- There are institutions where instruction (academic affairs) and student services are integrated and work hand in hand. I have been fortunate at my current institution for the past 10 years to have had a solid relationship with the current and former VPSA and to blend our roles and responses to mutual challenges. I realize much of this is based on established relationships between individuals but our work is too critical to be segmented and I do not take for granted the ability to work in a dynamic environment where one of my greatest co-partners is the VPAA.
- I am the product of the … community college system. As an immigrant and first-generation college student I know first-hand the transformational impact of a college education and is one reason I value the access mission of the CC system, for it provides the opportunities that might otherwise not be afforded to underprepared, low socioeconomic, underrepresented, and underserved students.

### R17

- Student activism. We're seeing a minor resurgence, which I welcome, but I want us to be good at responding.
- Title IX compliance in general, and reducing gender-based violence. 'Nuff said.
- Black student success. Our student success efforts have been effective for all groups except black students. I [created] a new position to devote to this.
- (Yes, listed them again—they're both challenges and opportunities)
- Student interest in an opportunities to provide new leadership development opportunities.
- Students in general. We have some great ones.
- Development: I have a $250,000 ask pending and hope for more.

### R18

- Students—after 37 years the excitement, the joy, and challenge are about student learning, growth, and development.
- Organizational changes and challenges—a general manager's approach to building the right team of "subject matter experts," weaving these talents to greater heights to promote the university's mission and aspirations.
- Solving problems at all levels of the institution, especially with cabinet colleagues that cross all segments of university life and viability.
- For these reasons, I enjoy this work, [a] calling if you will, as much as ever, as it is a privilege to have a role that draws on so many aspects, interests, and abilities while never failing to expose my inadequacies.

**R19.** No response.

**R20.** No response.

**R21**

- Resilient students.
- Observing/learning about the transformative experience many students have in college.
- Talented and invested colleagues.
- Periodically when we get something "right" and students and/or the common good is served.
- The purposefulness of the core work.

**R22**

- Direct student engagement. Once a week I carve out a little time just to walk around the [union] which is where our student government, Greek life, and student org offices are located. I take pics with students, just chat with them, and engage. That is better than any cup of coffee.
- Reading about current issues in the field is also energizing. It helps me remember to always be a student of this discipline. That role is as critical as my role as a leader. This is my belief because in my estimation, lack of evolution by learning = lack of effective leadership.

**R23**

- I think the progress we are making in the social justice arena and in engaging students to be service and civil-minded. Today's students generally are excited to give back to the communities they live in and to get involved in service-related activities.
- I also think the progress we are making to ensure equitable rights of all students is encouraging. Specifically, I think the progress made to make campuses more welcoming and supportive of transgendered students, pregnant students and students with service animals are just a few that demonstrate the influence higher education has in our society.

**R24**

- The opportunity to effect social change through the students we educate and send forth into the world!
- The social justice commitment of our field.
- Working with colleagues all across the university who share our commitment to student learning and success.
- Great national community of student affairs.

**R25**

- I am still excited to see students learn, transform, and change.

- Having meaningful conversations.
- Collaborative efforts on meaningful conversations with colleagues and students about how to change culture.

**R26**

- I still enjoy master's students and watching them learn about and appreciate the professional life of a higher ed person.
- I also like working with the doctoral students we attract. They really do "get it" in both arenas and many are doing very good, useful work when they graduate. It is still exciting and fulfilling.

**R27.** What excites me is working in a community college where I am able to serve underrepresented, economically disadvantaged students for whom we can help make the "American Dream" a reality. Our world prospers, therefore.

**R28.** I continue to be impressed with the young professionals I encounter. They seem to have great enthusiasm and are so dedicated to providing an environment where students can be successful. The commitment of young professionals to continuing to broaden access to college is admirable.

**R29.** It's still the best job in the world to be surrounded by bright young minds each and every day—to be challenged and to be affirmed by what they are doing.

**R30.** Despite the fact that I am sleep deprived, I do what I do because I truly do believe in this work. I am inspired and motivated each and every day by the potential I see in young adults and the role I can play as they immerse themselves in experiences and opportunities that enable them to find, raise, and place their unique voices in the world in ways that are transformative.

**R31**

- Locally, I am excited about a new president and provost who understand the scholarship of learning and are deeply committed to creating a campus experience that integrates the life of our students. I also have a division full of colleagues committed to best practices and application of the scholarship of our profession.
- I am excited about the demographic shifts that will happen in this country that will require/compel college and university campuses to consider strengthening cultural competencies.
- I am excited about some of the work coming out of AAC&U related to social responsibility and high impact educational practices (also NSSE data).
- How learning outcomes and assessment are holding us more accountable to the work we should be doing.

**R32.** Interacting with students, hearing about their aspirations and accomplishments, seeing the impacts that they are making on each other, our campus and our world is truly inspirational. And being able to facilitate this daily is an honor.

**R33**

- I love my job. I love the diversity of the challenges and the opportunities to make a real difference in the lives of our students, many of whom are first generation and international. I love "being in charge" in that I can influence a large sector of the institution and the student experience. I like having the opportunity to hire smart, capable, talented people who buy into a vision of a student affairs division committed to growth, development, and graduation of an incredibly diverse student body.
- I am in year three of my position. I have spent a good deal of time, energy, and capital getting the division "straightened out" due in part to the fact that it didn't have leadership for almost three years before me. Only this year have I really started to think about larger, more long-term issues, such as articulating the curriculum of our work. Another exciting aspect of my job is the strong possibility that a res hall project may soon be approved with shovels in the ground by spring. That is a great opportunity.

**R34.** After 30 plus years in the field I still love my work. Students are by and large fabulous and the opportunity to impact their developments, learning and success is incredibly rewarding and fulfilling. We still have much good work to do and it is feeling committed to that good work and impacting each new generation of future leaders of the world that keeps me going!!!

**R35.** The same thing that has always kept me going: the daily opportunities—on both a micro and macro level—to make a positive impact in the lives of students.

**R36**

- Positively impacting the lives of students.
- Helping to shape policy and practice in the academy to improve postsecondary education.
- This one keeps me up at night and also excites me: There continues to be a inexcusable paucity of African-American men graduating with their bachelor's—this is unacceptable and our institutions have the ability to move this needle IF we are genuinely committed to doing so.
- The academy continues to be at the center of wide-ranging sociopolitical issues that are shaping the world.
- Making sure to keep a long lens and remain focused on long-term impact and not get tripped up by current obstacles.

- Developing talented and deeply committed staff members is immensely rewarding.
- This one excites me and is also very troubling: [At my institution] being 1 of 2 female officers (out of 14) is inordinately challenging and difficult.

### R37

- The chance to positively impact the lives of hundreds and thousands of students over time through policy and program decisions, if I am willing to responsibly exercise my power, authority, influence and voice, as well as bring my authentic/fearless self to work.
- The strong belief (and reality!) that education remains one of the most impactful ways to improve quality of life for individuals, families and communities, as well as promote health and social justice.
- That the survival and thriving of our states, our country and our globe is predicated on providing higher education to as many of your youth and young adults as possible, to ensure a lively and effective democracy and a productive, well-balanced life (i.e., the goals of a liberal education).
- That the emerging problems facing the world for the future will require only more innovative problem-solving, critical thinking, the ability to communicate effectively, the responsible use of data analytics, and the capacity to work well in diverse teams—all skills that higher education is uniquely positioned to develop in citizens and leaders.
- The potential for higher education to be catalysts and drivers for positive change with conscience in other major institutions across U.S. society—should we wish to embrace our responsibility—including health care, K–12 education, justice system, media.
- The opportunities that come from engaging with hopeful individuals through our engagement with students and in our collaborations with faculty and in our interactions with donors/investors and in our partnerships with other constituents who also care about higher education!
- That I am part of a vibrant, dynamic, ever-evolving environment that promotes lifelong learning and growth for myself—if I am open to being changed—and can allow me to continually improve my leadership capacities, both through failure and through success.

### R38

- Breakthroughs when people find ways to connect with others who are ready to work in new ways (we're getting there in some corners of [my institution])!
- Possibilities of harnessing analytics (learning, predictive, etc.) to inform student success practice. We have SO MUCH data on SO MANY things that it's unethical NOT to use it in service of student success.

**R39.** The next generation of practitioners gives me much hope and excites me. They are much better prepared for this work than we were at the same points in our careers. That's a testament to our generation, though, who have made the commitment to provide our younger colleagues with a breadth and depth of professional development not available to most of us now in the senior positions. They recognize the challenges we will bequeath to them and are actually energized to find solutions to them. Bless their hearts!

**R40.** Student success. Looking at different options to help students be successful and graduate from credit for prior learning, improvements in development education, and competency-based learning. Faculty, staff, and administrators seem to understand that the ways we have been doing business cannot be sustained because it isn't working for all students.

**R41**

- All the successes we have had and the potential for more. As a community college SSAO, I'm looking at metrics such as retention and graduation rates and student grades. By using student learning and development theory to guide our work, we have already moved the needle in the right direction.
- I love the opportunity to develop staff (their own knowledge base, using literature, their leadership skills), and determine and execute strategic priorities.
- We are not on the sidelines here, and we shouldn't be anywhere.

**R42.** I love the students I work with and the people with whom I work. They inspire me and keep me believing that we can raise this sinking ship.

**R43.** The ability to have a real presence on a campus, be a role model and make an impact for many years to come with our students.

**R44**

- There are two unrelated things that keep me going: resilience and innovation.
- During my 20+ years in higher ed, I have seen a great deal of resilience in the field in general, as well as with individual professionals and students. It often amazes me to hear of the remarkable achievements of our students despite nearly insurmountable challenges. The same is true for the field. Sweet Briar College is a great example—it is the Lazarus of higher education. This resilience is a testament to the human spirit, persistence, and optimism gives me hope that we will continually be able to overcome the challenges that lay ahead.

- Innovation also keeps me going as it demonstrates that there are unique approaches to the challenges of the day. But, more importantly, it satisfies my intellectual curiosity. Trying to find innovative solutions to issues is almost like a game. It requires us to pull on a variety of skills and knowledge and to also examine the issue in a different way. I guess it feeds my inner geek.

**R45**

- What keeps me going is being active to mitigate those risks.
- The insane amount of new construction/renovation money that's come my way for student support.
- Putting to rest traditional student affairs that has historically bifurcated curricular and co-curricular life in favor of a far more integrated model.
- Expansion of the diversity of our students.
- A clear vision to my retirement!

**R46**

- Our amazingly talented students.
- Diversity commitments and progress.
- Civic engagement and leadership.
- Working with great colleagues who are deeply committed to doing good work.

**R47.** The growing recognition of the effect of student affairs, its importance to student success, our collective capacity for conveying care, the growing number of departments and individuals who wish to partner with us .... the growing appreciation for the value of our work.

**R48.** At this point in my career, truly being able to use my experience to mentor (and hopefully lead) staff to seek new opportunities to support student success.

**R49**

- Our students, my staff, and college staff.
- Opportunities to interact and engage with our students.
- Change—new projects which are exciting ... new building projects, other new initiatives which will benefit our students.

**R50**

- Historic stand of creating culture and being a model for society.
- Vision and energy of colleagues and students.

- Would much rather be in the middle of the conflict than standing on the sidelines.
- Learn something every day, not to mention I am having fun.

### R51

- Students—you see them grow before your eyes and then the ones that have gone on form the network to support the next generation of students. Today I had coffee with one young woman who was a "self reported burn out" her freshman year. Now she is a senior anticipating applying to a social work program for next year and she is a student manager in the union and has learned incredible leadership in that role and a sense of responsibility for others. I introduced her to three alumni in 1 hour's time and all are going to help her think of "and what next."
- That web of people that supports others but also makes extraordinary contributions to the community and to our knowledge ... that is what keeps me going.

**R52.** The opportunities to connect academic learning and cocurricular experience are broader than ever before (in my experience). Work on "microcredentialing" or "digital badging" on career development skills, well-being and flourishing, student leadership and initiative management, intergroup dialogue, and other areas is bubbling up at my institution, and students are embracing it. We are having energizing conversations with faculty, with employers, and with academic administrators, and there is a sense of positive momentum here. I am enthused because this movement seems to highlight the role of student affairs as the "Enriching Integrator," as suggested by Garland and Grace in their 1993 monograph, and makes clear that student affairs work can be at the center of creating a truly rich and integrative learning experience for our students.

### R53

- The opportunity to truly do work around equity and access to postsecondary education.
- Helping students find their voice.

# The Jossey-Bass Student Leadership Competencies Database

How do you know you're teaching the leadership skills your students will need?

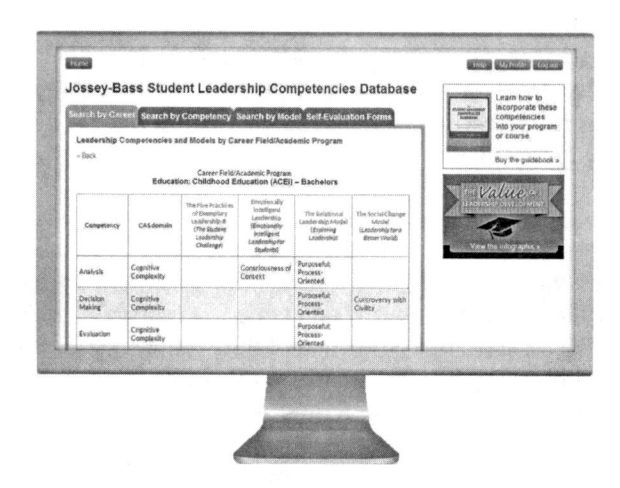

Bridge the gap between leadership development and career preparation by teaching your students the skills required by their academic programs and future career fields. Use this free online tool, covering the four major models of student leadership development, to align your course or program to accreditation requirements.

Try it now at www.josseybass.com/go/studentleadershipcompetencies

**JB JOSSEY-BASS**
A Wiley Brand

Jossey-Bass is a registered trademark of John Wiley & Sons, Inc.